THE STANISLAVSKY TECHNIQUE: RUSSIA

A Workbook for Actors

MEL GORDON is Associate Professor of Drama, Tisch School of the Arts, New York University. He is the author of *LAZZI: the Comic Routines of the Commedia dell'Arte* and has recently edited the volumes *Dada Performance* and *Expressionist Texts*. He was formerly the Associate Editor of *The Drama Review*.

THE STANISLAVSKY TECHNIQUE: RUSSIA

A Workbook for Actors

by

Mel Gordon

APPLAUSE THEATRE BOOK PUBLISHERS

THE STANISLAVSKY TECHNIQUE: RUSSIA

Library of Congress Cataloging-in-Publication Data

Gordon, Mel.
    The Stanislavsky technique.

    (The Applause acting series)
    Bibliography: p.
    1. Stanislavsky method. 2. Theater—Soviet Union—History—20th century. I. Title. II. Series.
PN2062.G67 1987   792'.028   87-17451
ISBN 0-936839-08-2 (pbk.)

Applause Theatre Book Publishers
211 West 71st Street
New York, N.Y. 10023
(212) 595-4735
Distributed in the UK and Europe by:
Applause Theatre Books LTD
All rights reserved. Printed in the U.S.A.

First Applause Printing, 1988

This book is dedicated to my teachers,
Stella Adler, Lee Strasberg, and Beatrice Straight.

Not only did they disseminate the teachings of Stanislavsky,
Vakhtangov, and Michael Chekhov in America,
they also, in their art, demonstrated its power and efficacy.

CONTENTS

ACKNOWLEDGMENTS

As I was forewarned, the simplest and shortest books are the most difficult to write. Therefore, I feel a very special gratitude to my editor Michael Earley, who worked tirelessly and with painstaking care to keep this book simple and structurally sound.

I am indebted to many people who helped me secure scarce materials and untangle seemingly unsolvable problems in translation and interpretation. Their generosity included, not only access to their private archives and memories, but technical and artistic advice in this project. They are Georgette Boner, the late Blair Cutting, Bobby Ellerman, Eleanor Faison, Nina Kerova, Alma Law, Felicity Mason, Mala Powers, Deirdre Hurst du Prey, Rose Raskin, Seinya Silverman, the late Vera Soloviova, Anna Strasberg, Slava Tsukerman, and Benjamin Zemach.

In addition, several of my students at New York University's Tisch School of the Arts assisted me in gathering information and conducting interviews. Among them are Cathy Bergart, Jeanee Collins, Emil Dimitroff, Barney Hanlon, Elany Portafeskas, and Denise Schneider.

INTRODUCTION:
THE STANISLAVSKY DEBATE

The art and practice of acting is still turning on the revelations and teachings of Konstantin Stanislavsky. In many ways, Stanislavsky's international influence has grown appreciably, not diminished, since his death in 1938. Now, fifty years later, the shadow of this Russian theorist and director probably looms even larger over the stages and rehearsal halls of the contemporary theatre than at any point in his own lifetime. And today, long after the impact of Meyerhold, Brecht, Artaud, Grotowski, and a dozen other innovative directors and thinkers on acting have run their course in academic and performance circles, it is virtually impossible to discuss modern acting or actor training without first mentioning Stanislavsky's contribution and those of his Russian and American disciples. Together, they have created a tradition that is inescapable and fundamental for anyone approaching the subject of acting.

Yet, a vehement, and seemingly inexhaustible, debate still rages over the value and exact meaning of Stanislavsky's work. From the Dom Kino actors' club in Moscow to the West Bank Cafe on Manhattan's Theatre Row—and at all points in between where actors, directors, and playwrights gather for drinks and serious shop-talk—a surprisingly like minded set of questions, inquiries, interpretations, misconceptions, and challenges to Stanislavsky's System of actor training can be heard nonstop.

At any of these typical gatherings, one can pick out of the conversations the same enduring questions that provoke this ongoing debate: "Does Stanislavsky have any relevance today?" "Isn't his teaching primarily linked to the heavy realism of Ibsen, Chekhov, and Odets?" "Don't Stanislavsky's acting preparations unnecessarily burden the innately talented performer?" "What did Stanislavsky actually want from his Moscow Art players anyway?" "Was he for the ensemble or for the uncharted individual expression of each actor?" "How does Stanislavsky's System relate to Broadway and American theatre conditions, where performers have only five or so weeks of rehearsal, or to Hollywood, where film actors often have no more than a few hours to quickly rehearse and block a scene before being placed on their marks?" "Didn't Stanislavsky eventually reject the actor's dependence on his personal memories in favor of imagination and physical movement?" "What were the master's final ideas on technique?" "Isn't the problem of understanding Stanislavsky's writings and books mostly related to inadequate editing and translation in their English language versions?" "Don't the celebrated performances by non-Stanislavskian trained actors, like John Gielgud and Laurence Olivier, disprove the need for intense internal work?" "Which of the contemporary (and competing) disciples of the Russian master correctly interpreted Stanislavsky's theories: Evgeni Vakhtangov, Michael Chekhov, Ilya Sudakov, Mikhail Kedrov, or Vasily Torporkov in the

Soviet Union; Lee Strasberg, Stella Adler, Sandy Meisner, or Bobby Lewis in America?" "And, if he were alive still today, which acting teacher (including those above) would Stanislavsky himself most approve?"

The "Stanislavsky debate" among actors, directors, and teachers continues to be hotly contested to this day for two major reasons: 1) the Stanislavsky System's obvious importance in developing actor training programs at universities and in independent studios, and 2) because few of the above questions (as well as a dozen or so others) can be easily or fully answered by the available literature on Stanislavsky, his adherents, and detractors.

* * * *

The Stanislavsky Technique: Russia is intended to resolve some of the enduring problems and misunderstandings about Stanislavsky and his System. It is a book primarily for actors and people who work in the theatre. It focuses on the practical and playable aspects of the System's training, particularly in terms of exercises.

Although a great deal of factual information on Stanislavsky, Vakhtangov, and Michael Chekhov is presented here, this book in no way should be seen as a scholarly treatise or as a purely academic undertaking. And since there are over two hundred books and articles on Stanislavsky, which analyze the biographical and theoretical foundations of the man and his System, *The Stanislavsky Technique* takes a different approach. It discusses and clarifies the evolution and creative work of the System from a more objective and impartial perspective. In this sense, this book is meant to be a practical companion—or correlative—to the other printed works, especially Stanislavsky's own *An Actor Prepares*. Relying on materials from many sources, particularly private interviews and untranslated or unpublished writings, *The Stanislavsky Technique* provides a simple history of the development of Stanislavsky's System and descriptions of the acting exercises that were taught in various workshops and studios beginning in 1911. More than anything, it investigates the relationship between the life and career of Stanislavsky and his revolutionary discoveries in actor training. The constant transformation in Stanislavsky's thinking and methods were very often linked with his changing roles as an actor, director, writer, and teacher at the Moscow Art Theatre between 1897 and 1938. Also included here are complementary biographical accounts and studio work of Stanislavsky's two most influential Russian disciples, Evgeni Vakhtangov and Michael Chekhov.

HOW TO READ THE EXERCISES

In his 1925 history of the MAT First Studio, Pavel Markov called Stanislavsky's pupils "exercise mad." In a way, it is an apt description of Stanislavsky himself, his System, and the work of his disciples. Exercises, improvisations, and études (directed improvisations or scenes) were the means by which the System, in all its interpretations and reformulations, could school the modern actor and prove itself as a natural and teachable method of acting and actor training.

Although Stanislavsky, Vakhtangov, and Michael Chekhov left published records of their theories and training techniques, none of these could be construed of as "how-to-do" manuals. Instead, general classroom ideas and suggested physical work were used to illuminate their texts and articles. In some cases, exercises that were printed for a reading public never seemed to be practiced in their studios or schools. Their real "exercise madness" normally was limited to practical usage in the living classroom.

The exercises gathered here, with few exceptions, are descriptions of the actual actor training techniques of Stanislavsky, Leopold Sulerzhitsky (the First Studio's artistic head), Vakhtangov, and Michael Chekhov as recorded in studio transcriptions, student biographies, interviews, and other printed accounts. Some of the work requires partners or observers; but all of it originates with exercises that directly connect the Russian masters' teachings to their pupils and performers.

The exercises themselves follow the appropriate chronological chapters, except in two places (Chapters One and Six) where actual physical work does not apply. Although there are a large number of these exercises and études (between forty and eighty in each chapter), the total numbers are not exhaustive. Each of the teachers invented or practiced many more in their studios. In my selection, I have chosen exercises which best illustrate individual techniques while avoiding those that are repeated elsewhere in the book. For instance, in the several official and private archives of Michael Chekhov in Moscow, Zurich, New York, and Los Angeles, over 600 separate exercises have been identified in transcriptions. From these, I have chosen 100 which best typify the basic classroom assignments in Chekhov's workshops.

The listing of exercises in any one chapter does not necessarily imply the use of all of them on a typical day, week, or semester. Normally, three or four exercises would comprise a full acting period. Sometimes, however, a single exercise or étude could take up an entire afternoon—for example, Vakhtangov's exercises in Public Solitude. Generally, the 50 or so exercises in a chapter might constitute a two-year regimen of course work. Naturally, the exercises could be performed in various new ways and combinations today. All the teachers of the System believed in a practical and fluid method of training actors.

In addition to the exercises, I have included a Glossary of

Terms and Course and Program Outlines of the System at the end of the book. This will enable the reader to identify technical terminology that has sometimes caused misunderstandings in discussions of Stanislavsky. All the terms used in the text and exercises that begin with a capital letter (*e.g.*, Affective Memory) are further explained in the Glossary. The Outlines will give the reader an idea how the exercises were combined into a complete program of study.

CHAPTER ONE

STANISLAVSKY'S EARLY YEARS AND THE MOSCOW ART THEATRE

I have lived a variegated life, during the course of which I have been forced more than once to change my most fundamental ideas.

Konstantin Stanislavsky, *My Life in Art*, 1924

FROM ALEXEYEV TO STANISLAVSKY

Stanislavsky was born Konstantin Sergeyevich Alexeyev in 1863, less than two years after the final abolition of serfdom in Russia. ("Stanislavsky" was a surname he would adopt at twenty-five.) Although his family was known for their extensive land holdings and wealth from the manufacture of gold and silver braiding for military decorations and uniforms, the Alexeyev clan was directly descended from serfs themselves. Only Stanislavsky's maternal grandmother, Marie Varley, a touring French actress, came from an artistic background.

1

The nine Alexeyev children grew up in an environment that mingled superstition with modern, liberal thinking. The young "Kostya" was raised by a peasant nanny and educated by a university trained governess. An obsessive fear of sickness, however, even of the common cold, and of premature death developed into life-long patterns for many of the Alexeyevs, including the frequently disease prone Kostya. Stanislavsky's mother sometimes slept in a special room in the estate's stables, believing fumes from horse manure had curative powers. The children were not even allowed to walk near a hospital, so great was the Alexeyev's terror of contagion.

When one of Stanislavsky's brothers was christened with a grandfather's name, the grandfather—as the old man himself had once predicted—died soon after. Although the family custom of naming children after living relatives ceased then, the closeness of death and its mysteries had taken root in the youngest Alexeyevs. To calm the children down when they became hysterical over the thought of mortality, the governess Evdokya Snopova revealed that there was a secret elixir of life: one drop on the tongue and you stay young and healthy forever; with two drops, you never die. The existence of such a powerful potion seemed so convincing that the children's mood immediately changed to playful excitement. Snopova taught them all kinds of make-believe diversions, where the children took on the roles of people long dead or powerful figures from far away worlds. The children's games grew into elaborate theatricals given on birthdays and holidays. And it is here that Kostya began to make the magical—and probably unconscious—link between health, immortality and the theatre.

Before 1861, on many Russian estates, talented or good-looking serfs were drilled by amateur directors for comic or musical performances. With the freeing of the serfs in the early 1860s, this entertainment quickly died out, but the amateur theatrical impulse it inspired—as well as the theatre buildings constructed for these amusements—remained. The Alexeyev family, like many other cultured Russians, mounted their own miniature spectacles. Snopova and other members of the large household directed evenings of specially written dramatic sketches.

Stanislavsky remembered one such occasion in vivid detail. To celebrate their mother's birthday, the Alexeyev children staged an elaborate fairy tale. The six-year-old Kostya eagerly took the role of Father Winter, dressed in a sheet of cotton and white wool. Placed on the stage in a fancy costume without reason or logical motivation—not even being told or knowing where to look—produced an intense physical discomfort. When the curtain rose, Kostya's Father Winter drew an instant round of applause that relieved the six-year-old of his distress. In his hands he held a "branch" made of rolled cotton. Warned to keep it far away from the flame of a lighted candle and only mime the action of putting it in the campfire, Kostya once again was filled with dreaded pangs of self-consciousness. Anxious thoughts flooded his mind, so he decided to make action real. The cotton branch immediately caught fire and the edge of his costume went up in flames. Stanislavsky remembered only being picked up and carried out of the theatre. Even in his youth, the danger of actual incineration was preferable to the horror of an actor standing awkwardly alone and without direction on the stage.

Encouraged by their mother, Elizaveta, the Alexeyev children became familiar with all aspects of the performing arts, particularly opera and circus. At eight, the shy Kostya suddenly became mad about circus. Once during an actual performance, he ran out into the ring to kiss a pink-leotarded equestrienne, much to the surprise of the family and ridicule of his brothers and sisters. With his brother, Volodya, at the piano, Kostya mounted his own circus show, called the "Konstantino Alexeyev Circus." Leading with his impressions of a ring-master directing the actions of a team of imaginary horses, Kostya also had his sisters jump through paper hoops as the bareback riders had done in the professional circus. But after demonstrations of the two-headed man, a human wheelbarrel, the disappearing clown, and a "dangerous" juggling routine, Stanislavsky's brother sometimes destroyed Kostya's fantasy by laughing and shouting at the spectators, "What silly fools! They imagine it's a real circus!" All this naturally invited Kostya's ire, but more interesting is how strongly the incident recorded itself in Stanislavsky's memory. This adolescent love of spectacle in its fine details and belief in the power of illusion would soon become trademarks of Stanislavsky's future work as a director.

Another of Kostya's passions was puppetry. Unable to duplicate the grandiose scenic displays of the circus or of his new love, the ballet, Stanislavsky turned to the marionette theatre. All the flats, moving scenery, and lighting could be constructed in miniature. Besides, wooden figures, unlike teasing brothers, could be controlled by a single creator and manipulated not to spoil the artistic spell. A large puppet stage was built, which soon attracted the interest of the neighboring children and adults. Inspired by live performances as well as pictures in books and magazines, Kostya mounted scenes and acts of famous plays that displayed catastrophic destruction in the finest detail.

Typical of his Lilliputian extravaganzas was Stanislavsky's first act of *The Corsair:* Beginning with a steady calm sea, a tiny ship sailed under the intense rays of a puppet sun. But as the sun disappeared, a storm arose with the coming of the night. The ship sank. In the churning cardboard waves, the heroes swam for their lives. From the shore, a lighthouse sent out its rotating beams of light. The storm lessened as the marionettes escaped from their watery grave. Just then dawn broke. In another production of Pushkin's *The Stone Guest,* Don Juan's descent into hell was so realistic that most of the marionette stage scenery went up in real flames. Once when the number of paying spectators grew more than the puppet-show hall could accommodate, the young impressario Stanislavsky moved his entire stage to a larger room. Later he realized that this ruined the evening. The increased scale for the audience became too great; the diminutive players and their actions could hardly be seen. The lesson for Kostya was not lost: greed can sometimes ruin art.

At fourteen, Stanislavsky started to keep a theatrical note-book of impressions and observations; much of it about his own self-doubts and difficulties on the amateur stage. These earliest reflections reveal a fascinating, analytical and mature understanding of the actor's basic problems. Its power lies in Stanislavsky's adolescent vanity and innocence. He primarily wanted to know what acting preparations were necessary to make an audience love and admire him.

In his first entry in September 1877, Stanislavsky wrote about two characters he created for an evening of one-acts. In the play *A Cup of Tea,* Stanislavsky emulated the acting of his favorite Moscow comedian Nikolai Muzil. Every rehearsal was a pleasure for him and on stage he felt a complete sense of ease and lightness as he imitated Muzil's eccentric interpretation. The audience applauded loudly at the presentation, but Stanislavsky's director thought little of his characterization, which caused the fourteen-year-old actor to wonder whether the spectators were in fact clapping for Muzil instead of him. The second comic piece, *The Old Mathematician,* proved absolutely torturous for Stanislavsky. Without a ready-made model, Stanislavsky based his character on patented routines and acting bits of ten other famous performers. Both in rehearsal and on stage, Stanislavsky felt empty and dull as the Old Mathematician. Clearly, the spectators did not care for Stanislavsky's character. But again Stanislavsky's director surprised him backstage by praising his acting in the *Old Mathematician* sketch as vastly superior to the Muzil imitation. As a teenager, Stanislavsky discovered one of theatre's most significant contradictions: what the actor may feel is not what the audience or director sees.

For sixty-one years, Stanislavsky kept diaries and journals of his theatre experiences. He relied heavily on them for inspiration and source material for his System. The simplest rehearsal situation could be the subject of a profound technical discovery, artistic reflection, or sharp aphorism. Nearly all of Stanislavsky's innovations were rooted in these private memorandums and observations. While directing French comedies and musicals at the Alexeyev family theatre, for example, the teenaged Stanislavsky realized that his most introverted sister always chose to play coquettes while his more outgoing sister passionately favored nuns. In the diary he recorded that actors have a tendency to play their opposites. During the same period, Stanislavsky discovered that a strong director can push the despairing and frustrated performer beyond fatigue and helplessness into a full emotional and intellectual release, a breakthrough. The lesson: the actor needs forceful direction.

THE ALEXEYEV CIRCLE AND FIRST PROFESSIONAL TRAINING

In 1877, the Alexeyev family announced the opening of their own amateur theatre group, the Vladimir Alexeyev Circle. It would soon be considered Moscow's finest non-professional company. For Stanislavsky, an indifferent student during his teens, the Alexeyev Circle became the natural focal point of his boundless energy. While rote memorization in the classroom appeared to be beyond his formidable intellectual capacities, no idea was too ridiculous or time-consuming for his character preparations. Once, to check the authenticity of his acting, Stanislavsky dressed as a tramp and went down to the railroad yards. Unrecognized by the station workers and his neighbors, he returned home, declaring the experiment a success. Another time, he roamed the estate disguised as a gypsy. As a kind of dramatic test one summer, Stanislavsky remained in his character for an entire day—acting exactly as his character would. When Stanislavsky's cousin, playing the father-in-law in the production, came to rehearse, Kostya started to run away, begging his "father-in-law" to leave him alone.

By Stanislavsky's eighteenth birthday, it was clear that his love of theatre was no longer that of a stage-struck dilettante. In 1881, he went to Moscow to study at a new acting academy founded by some members of the Maly Theatre, Russia's most important theatre. According to Stanislavsky, the training there was neither scientific nor suited to the individual performer. Any notion of acting technique or a formal curriculum was nonexistent. Students worked basically on scenes. Whenever an instructor thought a mistake had been made, he showed the pupil how to move his head or trill his "r"s. The students were merely drilled to duplicate their teachers' notions of acting. It was acting by imitation.

Three weeks after entering the Moscow conservatory, Stanislavsky left for a more professional education at the Maly Theatre itself. If acting was merely imitation, he thought, he might as well copy great performers at closer

hand. Although exceedingly handsome and tall now, Stanislavsky soon developed an odd reputation in Moscow social
circles for his physically awkward behavior. So clumsy was
Stanislavsky that, reportedly, when he entered a room all the
porcelain figurines and vases had to be removed lest he
knock them over. While dancing, he tipped over a palm
tree, on one occasion, and brought down a grand piano on
another. This embarrassing contrast between his assured
appearance and tension-filled body provided Stanislavsky
with a problem and special insight into acting that no graceful leading man could ever know.

At the Maly, Stanislavsky noticed that the best actors
came early to rehearsals and performances—sometimes as
early as two hours before their call. Unlike late-arriving
amateur divas, they did not experience a rush of energy by
keeping lesser actors and directors waiting. Stanislavsky
saw how the better actors rehearsed in full, not whispered,
tones; they did not "save" themselves for opening night.
Their performances on the stage appeared lively and fresh,
their actions seemingly unfolded for "the first time" night
after night. The "whispering" actors feared they would lose
this freshness in the rehearsal process. Somehow the better
performers knew how to overcome the dread of going stale
in a part. The greatest secret for Stanislavsky had to do with
inspiration. Beginning with his first stage experiences,
Stanislavsky learned, like most amateur actors, to pick up
inspiration from the auditorium, from the spectators. Naturally, the more unresponsive his audience, the weaker the
actor's performance. From a Maly actress, Stanislavsky

learned the "trick" of self-inspiration. Rather than playing to the house, he was told to find inspiration from his stage partner, to look deeply into the partner's eyes, not over them as was the custom. The eye contact that one makes in real life (and therefore on the stage) can be the source of the strongest unspoken communication between people.

SALVINI'S "OTHELLO"

Stanislavsky also followed closely the activities of visiting theatre troupes and actors. In 1882, the Italian tragedian Tommaso Salvini performed Othello in Moscow. It proved to be a turning point in Stanislavsky's life. Expecting to be bored by the Romantic "tricks" and histrionics of the aging Milanese, Stanislavsky instead saw Salvini's performance as a touchstone for all powerful, clearly drawn, beautiful and emotionally truthful acting. Salvini's first gesture and words burned themselves into Stanislavsky's memory. Here was an actor who had absolute control over his audiences. Previously, Stanislavsky had noted in his journals that a good actor could hold the complete attention of the house for seven minutes and no more; a typical performer for about one minute. The notebook equation did not apply to the sublime Salvini. Stanislavsky thought of Salvini as "a tiger of passion," a sculptor who could "mold" and transform the character of Othello into different statues of "flowing bronze." Pure artistry and human behavior, graceful movement and shocking emotionality was blended by Salvini into a breathtaking unity. It was not only Salvini's celebrated voice but his body itself that projected the most complicated and subtle of feelings. Stanislavsky wrote that the passion of Salvini's Othello was so visceral that it seemed as if "burning lava was pouring into his heart." Stanislavsky had now found a perfect model. When he learned that his idol came to the theatre three hours early to prepare himself emotionally, Stanislavsky was overjoyed. He immediately shaved off his goatee and trimmed his moustache in the Italian style. The young Russian actor began to look like Salvini.

"STANISLAVSKY," THE ACTOR

In 1888, the twenty-five-year-old Stanislavsky found himself in a difficult position. He was a business manager in his father's prosperous firm and a trustee of various Russian cultural societies. To his family and business associates, acting as an accomplished amateur was one thing, but performing on the commercial vaudeville stage was a disrespectable and unthinkable occupation, a form of cultural prostitution and social suicide. But Stanislavsky was determined to stake out a professional theatrical career. He had outgrown his amateur status. Appropriating the Polish-sounding name "Stanislavsky" from a retired actor he once admired, Konstantin Alexeyev was able to disguise his identity as well as create an exotic, foreign aura for his new stage persona. The adapted name even contained all the phonemes of "Salvini." Konstantin Stanislavsky was born.

Acting romantic bon vivants in slightly risqué French farces, Stanislavsky was both able to play on his looks and to put to use his acting experience. His double life of manager Alexeyev by day and actor Stanislavsky by night proved challenging, but fed Stanislavsky's dire need to act before real audiences. One night his father and mother surprised him by showing up at one of his performances. The next day Stanislavsky's father scolded him like a schoolboy. But seeing his son's resolve, the senior Alexeyev offered him funding for the development of his own semi-professional art theatre. It was to be called the Society for Art and Literature.

THE SOCIETY FOR ART AND LITERATURE

To inaugurate the Society and to give it some instant celebrity, a noted professional director and playwright, Alexander Fedotov, was hired in the summer of 1888. Fedotov's influence on Stanislavsky's development would be immeasurable. To start, he taught the young actor to find his character models from living people, not from imitating other actor's interpretations. This simple advice unblocked a huge barrier in Stanislavsky's work. He no longer had to follow, technically, in the shadows of the great performers. Suddenly he felt free to experiment and create his own preparatory techniques, something he had impulsively done since childhood, but was now sanctioned by Fedotov. Stanislavsky quickly realized that a relaxed body could make smaller, more refined and subtler gestures. Tension interferes with movement. One way of reducing the muscular tension in the body was to create a small area of tactile pain.

By pressing his fingernails into his palm or putting a stone in his shoe, Stanislavsky discovered the rest of the body automatically relaxed.

Under Fedotov's direction, Stanislavsky's revelations filled notebook after notebook. One well-known acting innovation of his was the idea of using opposite character traits—another childhood invention: "When you play an evil man seek out where he is good; when you play a young man seek out where he is old." Working for these strong contrasts resulted in a denser, more varied, and truthful performance. Yet as exciting as some of his concepts were, many of Stanislavsky's acting problems were not so easily resolved through this working on himself. Onstage, he still had a tendency to rely on stage clichés, especially in heroic parts. He began to understand that his preference for historical and character roles was, in part, a product of his introverted personality; in other words, a mask. He was frightened to reveal too much of himself, and yet knew no way around the fear. Also, too many ideas and theories led to self-consciousness before a performance and consequential stage fright. Stanislavsky's strongest and most curious discovery, however, resulted from his courtship of the actress Masha Perevoshchikova. Being in love filled him with a special energy and lightness that made every technique for relaxation and characterization superfluous. Stanislavsky could not get over the fact that his acting, in every instance and role, improved markedly when he was in love. Yet when the ardor cooled, Stanislavsky's old acting problems returned and he knew of no way to regain the magical state.

SAXE-MEININGEN'S TROUPE IN MOSCOW

In 1890, Stanislavsky saw the second Moscow tour of the Duke of Saxe-Meiningen's theatre company. When the German players visited Russia in 1885, Stanislavsky had little interest in their historical reconstructions of the epochs of the classic repertoire or the naturalistic scenic decor. Some Russian critics, like Vladimir Nemirovich-Danchenko, thought that the Meiningen Players, with their emphasis on spectacle, often reduced the Shakespearean and German Romantic texts to utter dramatic simplicity or unintelligibility. But their use of genuine properties and costumes astonished the Moscow audiences. Every production was designed as a theatrical time machine: *Julius Caesar* was less an Elizabethan play or even a nineteenth-century interpretation of it than an excursion into the world and artifacts of first-century Rome. The scenic and lighting effects of vanishing ghosts and moonlight alone created a frightening realistic illusion.

Stanislavsky was especially impressed with the sparks that flew from the clash of real fifteenth-century swords. Only the German performers' voices were hopelessly thin and weak, Stanislavsky wrote in his journal. The military-like discipline of the Meiningen troupe, under Ludwig Chronegk's autocratic direction, also caught his attention. To begin with, the striking of a triangle summoned performers to rehearsal. Any actor late to rehearsal was subject to replacement. Order and efficiency pervaded the entire backstage area. Inattention, sloppiness, "bohemianism," hysteria—all the commonplace hazards of the Russian theatre—were absent here. Saxe-Meiningen's company with its fine detail and artistic discipline became a model for Stanislavsky's next venture: directing for the Society of Art and Literature.

STANISLAVSKY DIRECTS

Learning his craft now with great care, Stanislavsky, during the next six years from 1890 to 1896, became regarded as Moscow's most interesting and modern stage director. Imitating the example of Saxe-Meiningen, he mounted a lavish production of *Uriel Acosta,* a melodrama about an apostate Jew in seventeenth-century Amsterdam, complete with elaborately choreographed crowd scenes and huge, but historically inaccurate, set pieces. It was a great success with the Moscow public. For a production of *Othello,* Stanislavsky travelled to Venice for original artifacts, costume and set designs. Both director and star of *Othello,* he knew enough about the tricks of theatre to darken the stage during the monologues of a poorly acted Iago. Gerhart Hauptmann's and Henrik Ibsen's Moscow premieres were given under the auspices of Stanislavsky, who quickly discovered that a director can easily dominate his actors but often without getting any creative results. His spectacular production of Monk Lewis' *The Bells,* a British melodrama made famous by Henry Irving, became the scenic high point of the Society's existence. The bedroom of an inn magically transformed into a dream-like court room during a brief blackout. Watching from the wings as his actors crawled to their marks, Stanislavsky laughingly marveled at his ability to astound an audience.

In the first months of 1897, however, several of the Society's productions failed miserably. A dark mood hung over the performers and director. Something essential had been lost. In the spring, Stanislavsky received a letter from Vladimir Nemirovich-Danchenko, a Russian critic and dramaturg from the Maly Theatre. It was an invitation to form a new professional theatre company, different from all the existing ones. The problem with the Society of Art and Literature's work was clear; even the most talented director could not continue to inspire amateur actors in season after season. Another artistic approach had to be tried.

THE CREATION OF THE MOSCOW ART THEATRE

On June 22nd, 1897, Nemirovich-Danchenko and Stanislavsky sat down in the Slavansky Bazaar Restaurant in Moscow and began one of the most celebrated eighteen-hour talks in the history of the theatre. It resulted in the formation of the Moscow Art Theatre (first called the People's Art Theatre; later the Moscow Art and Popular Theatre; finally the Moscow Art Theatre [MAT]). The start of their conversation dwelled on what both despised in the contemporary theatre of Moscow: its lack of acting discipline, especially in the rehearsal period, which in itself was far too short; the star system with its phony tricks and histrionics; performers' unchecked tendencies to overact; predictable and uninspired direction; hackneyed and overused flats and scenic design; the held curtain, which delayed most performances for nearly forty-five minutes; and a stale dramatic repertoire.

Their blueprint for the MAT was simple: it would run counter to all of the above. First and foremost, each actor would be treated like an artist. Along with respect, the MAT artists would receive clean and spacious dressing rooms, a library, a large green room, a club and social room complete with newspapers and chess tables. Once chosen for the company, the actor would be part of a democratic ensemble. The actors lived by the motto, "Today Hamlet, tomorrow an extra, but even as the extra the actor must be an artist." Stanislavsky repeated the dictum of Michael Shchepkin, Russia's famous classical actor: "There are no small parts, only small actors." Although the actor was the active element in a theatre production, both Nemirovich-Danchenko and Stanislavsky agreed that everything—the set, the lighting, the music, the direction, and the mise-en-scène—would serve the play's thesis.

An entire year passed before the MAT took shape in the early months of 1898. Time was spent raising operating funds and recruiting actors from the Society of Art and Literature and Nemirovich-Danchenko's private acting school. For their inaugural production, Nemirovich-Danchenko attempted to persuade Anton Chekhov, the already well-known short story writer, to release the rights for his first major play *The Seagull*. But Chekhov felt a more established theatre could mount a better production of it and he refused Nemirovich-Danchenko's request.

THE MAT'S FIRST SEASON

By the summer of 1898, the MAT selected Alexei Tolstoy's *Czar Fyodor* in place of *The Seagull*. An historical melodrama set in Russia's sixteenth-century, *Czar Fyodor* was based on the court intrigues of the boyars around a powerless czar. The controversial play had been banned by the Russian censors for three decades because of its political content. Yet Nemirovich-Danchenko managed to receive official approval for a production of *Czar Fyodor*. This triumph over the Czar's censors alone created an interest in the MAT's activities among Moscow's curious intelligentsia. Other theatregoers were more reserved about Stanislavsky's venture.

Rehearsing and living on an estate in Pushkino, outside Moscow, the young MAT actors experienced the most intensive and exciting summer of their lives. More than an ensemble of actors, the MAT emerged as a spiritual collective as each performer cooked or cleaned before and after the nine hours of daily rehearsals. The troupe declared that since they hated the falsehood of the stage, they equally opposed the hypocrisies of life. An actor could not create truthfully in the theatre without incorporating a sense of truth and simplicity into his everyday life. Twelve of the MAT members married during those halcyon months.

Now preparing for *Czar Fyodor,* Stanislavsky toured the Volga area, scouting out sixteenth-century objects and designs to use in his production. Groups of actors were led through impenetrable forests to ancient churches and monasteries unspoiled by the manners and fashions of contemporary Russia. There, the architecture, furniture, and clothing of Fyodor's era served as inspirations for the troupe. Each performer studied his costume and hand properties for character and movement ideas. Some of them attempted to base their physical appearance on icons. Others tried out gestures, gaits, movements, and vocal patterns that they imagined came out of the period. Stanislavsky wanted to go beyond the Meiningen Players in realizing historical accuracy. But, in the end, he lost trust in his young actors' private work. Stanislavsky showed nearly every performer exactly how his character should move and behave.

When *Czar Fyodor* opened on October 14th, 1898, the Moscow critics and audience were, at first, skeptical, then stunned. The first act unfolded with Stanislavsky's typical bag of theatrical tricks and special sense of humor: servants throwing imaginary dishwater into the audience, noble boyars secretly stealing the Czar's dishes and cutlery during dinner, and so forth. But during the second act, a new feeling enveloped the spectators' perception: this is the way old feudal Russia must have been. The undulating sound of church bells, the actor's heavy costumes and peculiar mannerisms, the consuming of real food and drink, the extreme

high and low levels of light, the detailed standing set pieces
and antique furniture, all combined to create a powerful and
unified mood that no one expected from a living performance. A vision of the past had come to life on the stage.

The Merchant of Venice and two other productions followed closely in their first season, but none gripped the
Moscow audience like *Czar Fyodor*. The critics harped in-
sistently on Stanislavsky's Yiddish-accented Shylock. Was
the MAT's search for historical realism an unconscious attempt to burlesque the classical repertoire, they wondered.
Then and only reluctantly, Chekhov gave Nemirovich-
Danchenko permission to use *The Seagull*—the Alexandrin-
sky Theatre in St. Petersburg had already made a mess of the
premiere. Unlike his partner, Stanislavsky was not enthusiastic about Chekhov's playscript. But after much thought,
Stanislavsky took on the project as a directorial challenge.

THE MAT BECOMES "THE HOUSE OF CHEKHOV"

The Moscow public had learned to enjoy Saxe-Meiningen's and the MAT's spectacles that brought classical and
historical plays into the theatrical embrace of the everyday
world with its petty details and naturalistic veneer. The poetic, exotic, and lofty atmospheres of these plays had been
brought into the realm of contemporary human behavior.
But for Chekhov's *The Seagull*, Stanislavsky decided to reverse this process: he would create a great spectacle of the
ordinary and banal. The smallest activity and interaction in

the text could be filled with dozens of scenic details and unspoken communications. Everyday life could be made totally exotic and, in doing so, a deeper psychological truth
between the characters could be mined. Compare Chekhov's opening stage direction of *The Seagull* with
Stanislavsky's directorial adaptation.

Chekhov's original text:
*The sun has just set. Yakov and other workmen are busy
on the stage behind the lowered curtain; sounds of hammering and coughing.*

Stanislavsky's prompt book:
*The play starts in darkness; an August evening. The dim
light of a lantern set on top of a post; distant sounds of a
drunkard's song; distant howling of a dog; the croaking of
frogs, the cry of a corncrake; the slow tolling of a distant
church-bell... Flashes of lightning, faint rumbling of
thunder in the distance. After the rise of the curtain a
pause of ten seconds. After the pause Yakov knocks,
hammering in a nail on the stage; having knocked the nail
in, he busies himself on the stage, humming a tune.*
(translated by David Magarshack)

Stanislavsky created a shock. His detailed realism transformed the most commonplace scene into a orchestrated display of minute effects. In some ways, it resembled his
courtroom scene in *The Bells* and even young Stanislavsky's
puppet productions. But without an historical frame of sixteenth-century Russia or fifteen-century Venice, the acting
looked different too. Something modern had been born.
Pauses in the dialogue—over a hundred are indicated in the

promptbook, but not in Chekhov's script—and long, piercing looks graphically demonstrated the sad, monotonous life of the characters. Instead of boring the spectators, these concentrated activities drew them into Chekhov's invisible world of the contemporary. Both the pauses and stares soon became the acting trademarks of the MAT.

Chekhov unintentionally gave the MAT the key to a new performance style: psychological realism. Here the hidden communications and conflicts between all classes and types of people—so imbedded in our normal daily experiences that we hardly notice them—were exposed. Chekhov's plays, as performed by the MAT, were not just naturalistic slices of life, but dynamic presentations that unmasked and exposed complicated human relationships and self-deceptions. With nearly all their external stage activity, including the smallest of gestures, poses, and character habits indicated by Stanislavsky, the MAT actors were forced to plumb the inner lives of their characters in order to create Chekhov's specialized and untheatrical mood and emotions. The script and the direction both restrained and delimited the expected histrionic behavior of the stage characters and therefore the actors. It seemed as if there was no "acting" or actors on the stage, only soulful individuals trapped in a gloomy, uneventful environment. Even the oddly retarded tempos of the MAT performers, without a heightened melodramatic rhythm or stagey climax, began to resemble the actual life of a Russian household.

Besides the internalized acting, all that was left to the spectators' eyes and ears were Stanislavsky's super-realistic lighting and sound effects that worked as a reflection or a contrast to the deep emotional longings of Chekhov's characters. So successful was *The Seagull* that the MAT immediately made the play's imprint their logo. Only the playwright himself seemed unhappy. Chekhov thought, for instance, that Stanislavsky's acting of the writer Trigorin was clownish and wrong-headed. The "mosquito-swatting" atmosphere, he wrote, very nearly ruined his play. But the triumph of *The Seagull* forced the playwright to slowly acknowledge that the MAT was the only theatre that could successfully stage his plays.

Much of the celebrated, out-of-doors, scenic effects that Stanislavsky created for Chekhov's plays were filled with a special mystery. But some of them were totally invented. According to Nemirovich-Danchenko, Stanislavsky knew absolutely nothing about the common details of nature. Once when Nemirovich-Danchenko criticized the accuracy of a scene designer's rendering of a pine tree, Stanislavsky became infuriated. Where would he find time and money to send the painter to southern Italy to sketch pine trees? A confused Nemirovich-Danchenko reminded his partner that pine trees were indigenous to Russia, and the Alexeyev estate was strewn with clumps of them.

Over the next seven years, the MAT produced nearly two dozen major plays, including Chekhov's *Uncle Vanya, Three Sisters,* and *The Cherry Orchard,* all of which were even more popular than *The Seagull.* The human melody of Chekhov's melancholic Russia struck a powerful chord in Moscow's theatre-going public. And the MAT was quickly referred to as the House of Chekhov. The total number of performances of Chekhov would run into the thousands, and for decades the original performers would continue to play the same roles. Only Maxim Gorky's *The Lower Depths,* produced in 1902, found equally enthusiastic audiences. A seemingly plotless drama about life in a Volga flophouse, *The Lower Depths* allowed the MAT players to demonstrate another mode of performance: Naturalism. Yet Stanislavsky's technique of using external properties to inspire the actor's mood remained exactly the same as it had for *Czar Fyodor* and the Chekhov plays. In addition, his detailed promptbooks revealed his old Saxe-Meiningen approach to direction. Every physical movement and intonation was worked out and given to the actor. Inattentive extras with a tendency to look into the audience were told to count the flowers or patterns on the backdrops.

By the time of *The Lower Depths,* the MAT had firmly established itself as a Russian institution. Its annual financial sheets were generally favorable—particularly after the Russian industrialist Savva Morozov bailed the MAT out of an early debt. Outside its newly refurbished theatre in Kamergersky Lane, servants and university students waited all night long around campfires to enter a morning lottery just for the privilege of purchasing precious MAT tickets. Once the numbers were announced, new queues of winners formed to buy available tickets. A season subscription to the MAT was a priceless item. The MAT now was home to a company of some three hundred performers and backstage workers, with its own Broad of Directors, stockholders, and patrons. A three-year training program for young actors had already been instituted. Apprenticed to experienced performers, or "nurses," each student-actor received classes in diction, voice, dance, fencing, and cultural studies. All this was years before Stanislavsky's own System became the focus of the MAT's actor training.

THE MAT'S FAME SPREADS

The reputation of the MAT and Chekhov had reached beyond Russia to Western Europe and North America. The novel and intensely rich style of acting was beginning to receive international interest. Even the MAT's abolition of curtain calls—in fact, of any audience applause—and principled treatment of late comers fascinated foreign writers. Slowly the MAT was reaching an artistic maturity. Only one problem remained: nearly half of the MAT productions failed critically. This disturbed Stanislavsky more than anyone else. Sometimes the acting grew stale or lost its spark; sometimes the noise and snow machines malfunctioned, producing an unexpected stage realism. The MAT Board of Directors, however, accepted this as the natural state of affairs. The death of Anton Chekhov in the summer of 1904, however, was an omen to Stanislavsky and Nemirovich-Danchenko that the MAT would evidently have to change its repertoire and methods, but this was for some time in the future.

In the first part of 1906, after the disastrous Russo-Japanese War and Czarist oppression at home, the MAT toured Germany and Central Europe. So impressive were their performances in Berlin that the Kaiser personally congratulated them. According to Stanislavsky's journals, the reclusive playwright Gerhart Hauptmann shouted during an intermission of *Uncle Vanya,* "No theatre has moved me like this. Those aren't people up there on the stage—they're artistic divinities!" Teasingly, German newspapers claimed the MAT was the first victory for Russia since its embarrassing military defeats in Asia the previous year. Everywhere the MAT players went, adoring fans followed. In staid Leipzig, Stanislavsky was carried on the shoulders of its citizens. One Viennese critic called the MAT, "perfection on stage."

Yet once the MAT returned to Moscow in the spring of 1906, the forty-three-year-old Stanislavsky underwent his greatest crisis, what may have amounted to a nervous breakdown. Like his direction, his acting became erratic. So unpredictable were his performances that three years earlier Nemirovich-Danchenko removed him from a production of *Julius Caesar.* Stanislavsky tried to explain to anyone who would listen that on some evenings he was filled with inspiration, but on others he felt totally empty. His friends tried to console him; this was the nature of the theatre, they said. Anyway, he just needed a long overdue vacation. Stanislavsky agreed. With his wife Masha, he retired to a Finnish resort. In a seaside dacha, Stanislavsky went over all of his notebooks for the next three months, attempting to find a way out of his personal malaise and artistic quandary.

CHAPTER TWO

LEOPOLD SULERZHITSKY, THE SYSTEM, AND THE FIRST STUDIO

People are afraid of thoughts. We live in a world of lies. The theatre can change this. And no one who has stood on the side of truth has ever regretted it.

Leopold Sulerzhitsky, 1914

Recuperating in Finland at the Baltic shore in the summer of 1906, Stanislavsky's six-month despair—from overwork and an exhausting tour—had not yet subsided. Although both he and the MAT had attained international stature as Russian institutions, acting for Stanislavsky had become a tedious and empty chore. Coyly executed gestures, phony expressions of naiveté, and all the stage tricks he could muster filled out Stanislavsky's German tour. Not one but all of his roles weakened as emotional inertia overtook his preparatory and stage work. Even Stanislavsky's

rich voice failed to register its full, trademarked tones of
lyrical sincerity and psychological candor. Like a self-conscious, amateur actor, he returned to rehearsing before a
mirror. Once, during a performance of *Uncle Vanya,* he lost
his powers of concentration; his mind kept pathologically
wandering back to an offstage conversation. Worst of all,
neither the MAT nor his audience seemed to care or notice
what he felt inside.

THE CREATIVE STATE OF MIND

During his convalescence, Stanislavsky searched desperately for answers. He examined his volumes of notebooks,
studied children at play, went for long walks, thought about
the successes and failures of his and other actors' careers.
He investigated these threads for a common bond. Finally,
it came to him. Every actor he respected shared certain
qualities: there was a kind of aura around them on the stage.
Audiences sensed something different about these performers. They were relaxed yet filled with a concentrated energy.
They were completely involved in the theatrical moment,
possessing an ease and liveliness that gave each of their roles
a special charge. The performances of these actors reminded
Stanislavsky of the absolute absorption and rapture children
feel when building sand castles—the same feeling that visual
artists have when finishing paintings, the purposefulness
that heightens adolescents' minds when writing love letters.
Time and place transform themselves. Actions and feelings
intensify, sublimate, wax artistic. Solely through the

strength of their faith and imagination, the child, the artist, and the lover transport themselves on to another, more creative plane.

Stanislavsky called this inspired artistic condition, the Creative State of Mind. It was the intense and expansive mood that writers and artists need to create. Exactly like love, it appeared to be instinctive yet remained a passion beyond the boundaries of any mental control. The Creative State of Mind, for most artists, could not be summoned at a moment's notice; it vanished as unexpectedly as it came. But great actors intuitively knew how to "create" it on the stage. In happier times, Stanislavsky also felt this state: suddenly his clumsiness and muscular tensions disappeared; he imperceptibly merged with his role and radiated a special energy that comes with being fully alive on the stage. This artistic fire, this sense of being that allows the actor to forget about the critical presence of the audience should be available to every actor. Yet only a celebrated handful could consistently reproduce it. One thing became evident to Stanislavsky, the potent Creative State of Mind could not be willed directly, so deeply was it imbedded in the mysterious and deeper recesses of the human mind. Perhaps hypnosis or physical exercises could stimulate and control it. Exploring and developing methods to release the actor's creative power would now preoccupy Stanislavsky.

In August of 1906 when Stanislavsky returned to Moscow, members of the MAT showed little interest in their director's discoveries. In fact, many of them thought that Stanislavsky was much better as an actor and director without his theories, which some found overly obsessive. And the more excited Stanislavsky became over his analysis and ideas, the more Nemirovich-Danchenko and the others feared for his mental balance. Every mature actor has a dry period, they warned. Accept it. Why change your working methods if everyone praises them? Still, Stanislavsky was determined to test his theories about the Creative State of Mind as best he could, by using himself as a guinea pig.

ENTER LEOPOLD SULERZHITSKY

Only one person seemed to understand the inspired fervor and significance of Stanislavsky's hypothesis. This was Leopold Sulerzhitsky, the MAT stage hand and jack-of-all-trades, who was Stanislavsky's junior by ten years. A colorful adventurer with a gift for storytelling, "Suler"—as he was re-christened by Maxim Gorky—was a favorite with the company, staff, and families of the MAT. Suler's life included stints in every kind of calling and occupation: he had been a fisherman in the Crimea, a merchant marine and sailor, a tutor and painter, a farmhand, a hobo, and a smuggler of pamphlets for the outlawed Social Democratic Party. A schoolmate of Lev Tolstoy's daughter, Suler converted to Tolstoy's social philosophy and militant pacificism in his twenties. Convicted as a conscientious objector and revolutionary, Suler served time in an army prison, a lunatic asylum, and was exiled later to Central Asia. Tolstoy was so taken with him that he declared Suler was "the purest man I ever knew.... All Three Musketeers rolled into one."

At the turn-of-the-century, Suler helped a group of Dukhobers emigrate from the Caucasus to Newfoundland in Canada. For two years, Suler helped them establish their Tolstoyan collective in the New World, learning in return their Eastern-influenced religious practices. So successful was Suler that Tolstoy recalled him to Europe, to assist with another commune in Cyprus. A bout of yellow fever, however, brought Suler to the Crimea, where he watched the MAT perform during their summer schedule. The MAT's artistic purity and uncanny ability to touch the audience's soul electrified Suler. Through his friend Gorky, he immediately made contact with Stanislavsky. Although he had no serious acting background, Suler was an accomplished painter and writer. His talent for music, singing, and dancing—Isadora Duncan would later praise him—might prove useful, Stanislavsky decided. Besides, Suler's open-faced naiveté and childlike manner were infectious. Suler was hired in the ill defined job category of "stagehand."

Curiously, only Suler, a theatre non-professional, understood Stanislavsky's excitement over his Baltic discoveries: the secret of great acting involves unearthing the mind's creative potential; the development of affective physical and psychophysical exercises must be the first path to a consistent awakening of the Creative State of Mind. Suler even offered a name for these exercises, yoga. This was the Sanskrit term that the Newfoundland Dukhobers called their daily spiritual and bodily regimen. Stanislavsky leaned forward in anticipation. Every morning, Suler recalled, the Dukhobers performed a meditation on their daily activities.

Seated in a relaxed position, each Dukhober focused on his hourly duties and visualized executing each work task in detail. These yogic exercises produced a calm and a certainty of purpose. The Dukhobers had become aware of Prana, a Hindu concept of the invisible life force that streams through all living things. Stanislavsky understood the importance of Suler's description. Prana was another name for the Creative State of Mind. A spring had been triggered in his imagination. Stanislavsky had found the beginnings of his System.

For some nine years, Stanislavsky and Suler became inseparable. As he had with Nemirovich-Danchenko a decade before, Stanislavsky spoke with his new collaborator for hours on end. Nearly every waking second—in Stanislavsky's dressing room, on the MAT's third floor—the two, one tall and other diminutive, exchanged ideas. Stanislavsky was giddy with new concepts and innovations. It was as if he were undergoing a second childhood. There was also something special about Suler. Even before their conversation about the Dukhobers, Stanislavsky impulsively persuaded Suler to jump in his carriage and come home with him when they first met in Moscow. This spontaneous gesture, like young Stanislavsky's running to kiss the circus equestrienne, proved to be a point of both personal and artistic transformation.

To the dismay and disapproval of Nemirovich-Danchenko, who had already threatened to resign and transfer to the Maly Theatre, Stanislavsky offered Suler a new position in the MAT, that of Stanislavsky's first assistant.

But claiming still to be a wanderer at heart, Suler warned that he might leave his new job at any time. This was a threat that Stanislavsky quickly accepted. He even paid Suler's salary out of his own pocket. Together, they replanned the MAT's future. Suler had novel ideas concerning the MAT repertoire and performance styles in addition to its rehearsal and training processes.

SEARCH FOR A SYMBOLIST ACTING TECHNIQUE

Since 1902, Russian Symbolist writers had criticized the realistic direction of the MAT productions. Valery Briusov, the noted Symbolist poet, declared that life had one reality and theatre another. What was the point of imitating life in the manner of Chekhov, even with the spectacular details of crickets chirping? The function of art, the Symbolists wrote, was to enter into the newly discovered and mystic worlds of the soul, in fact, to pierce the cardboard exteriors of reality. If all of this appealed to Stanislavsky's desire to create a deeper communication with his audiences, it also had an aesthetic attraction. Throughout the modern world, Symbolism was replacing Realism as a literary and dramatic trend. But in 1904 Stanislavsky's first attempt at directing a Symbolist play, three one-acts by Maurice Maeterlinck, failed dismally. Symbolism demanded a new performance technique.

Vsevolod Meyerhold, one of the founding actors of the MAT, left in 1902 to experiment with stylized productions of

the new Symbolist repertoire. Three years later, Stanislavsky asked him to return to the MAT as a director. A special Theatre Studio was created for Meyerhold and his
group. The summer presentations at Pushkino (the MAT's
original rehearsal retreat) and after were realized with visually grotesque mise-en-scènes, but the acting was devoid of
any inner life or fire. The actors' marionette-like movements
and hollowed-out voices perplexed Stanislavsky. Symbolist
acting should have touched the strings of the spectator's soul
with its profundity of meaning and technique. Meyerhold's
performers were merely directed mannequins, nothing more
than slow-moving statues. The MAT's further Symbolist attempts floundered from Stanislavsky's point of view. Then
in the fall of 1905, Meyerhold's Theatre Studio was formally
dissolved. But Stanislavsky's disappointment with him did
not prevent Meyerhold from continuing his acting and directorial experiments in other theatres and studios.

Suler pressed Stanislavsky once again for the inclusion of
Symbolist dramas. The fiasco associated with Meyerhold's
company, Suler pleaded, had more to do with Meyerhold's
tyrannical directorial methods than the plays themselves.
The spiritual depth of Symbolism necessitated a stronger,
more internalized style of acting. Direction that greatly emphasized the performer's use of his face and hands, the centers of Prana, Suler believed, would produce a higher form
of acting. The actors could now concentrate on the mysterious and internal aspects of their characters; except for
their faces and hands, they could ignore all extraneous corporal expressions and movement. Finally the actor's pure

soul could connect directly with the spectator's. In February 1907, Stanislavsky and Suler staged Knut Hamsun's *The Drama of Life* in this new and esthetically stiff fashion. Neither the critics nor the MAT audiences were pleased or emotionally affected by their radical attempt in soul communication.

While the older MAT members chortled in relief and Suler pouted in amazement at the failure of *The Drama of Life,* Stanislavsky showed no signs of his old malaise. In fact, he was more energized than ever. The problem was clear: by directing only the heads and hands of the actors, to the practical exclusion of any other moving part of their bodies, Stanislavsky and Suler had increased the muscular tension in their performers. This inhibited the actors from expressing their true and natural feelings; little wonder that spectators left unaffected and confused. If anything, *The Drama of Life* was a further proof of their acting theories.

In December of 1907, Stanislavsky produced one more Symbolist play, Leonid Andreyev's *The Life of Man,* which once again demonstrated his sure hand as a director of spectacle. During an early rehearsal for *The Life of Man,* Stanislavsky revealed the black velvet maquette to the performers. A black-costumed figure became lost in the stage model. Suddenly an idea occurred to the master—convert the evening into a magician's chamber of tricks and disappearing acts. The black box theatre was born. Originally Stanislavsky wanted to use black costumes to mask the natural and full movements of the actors. That way only those areas of the body, especially the faces and hands, could be uncovered at the director's will. For the first time, Stanislavsky's acting experiment worked. What looked like grotesque and stylized acting was wildly applauded for both its mise-en-scène and deep, forceful characterizations.

The Stanislavsky System had formally started with these experiments in Symbolist acting. The MAT, long called "the House of Chekhov," a theatre of intense psychological moods and minute realistic detail, now gave way to a theatre of soul-like truth and abstraction. It is important to note that Stanislavsky formed his acting workshops years and even decades after he produced his Chekhovian productions. In fact, the Stanislavsky System was first created to accommodate the problems of the Symbolist theatre. Had Stanislavsky remained a successful director of Chekhov and similar plays of realism and mood, there would have been no need to invent an acting methodology.

In 1908, Stanislavsky met in Normandy with the Belgian playwright Maeterlinck, the leading Symbolist writer. Stanislavsky needed to learn more about Symbolism for his production of Maeterlinck's masterpiece, *The Blue Bird*. It was during this trip that Stanislavsky became acquainted with Isadora Duncan—who in her free and spiritually-intense dances embodied what he wanted in acting—and her lover, Gordon Craig, the English stage designer and writer. Craig and Stanislavsky, agreed to direct a new, avant-garde production of *Hamlet* in Moscow at some future date. In the fall, Stanislavsky returned to Russia with still another notion: to build an artistic environment outside Moscow where spectators could spend time in nature, eating well, attending poetry and musical recitals as well as dramatic productions. Although this cultural garden never materialized, Stanislavsky's newest Symbolist-fantasy production of *The Blue Bird* completely caught the affections of Moscow's reviewers and audiences. But again something dissatisfied the restless director: the actors' work was inconsistent, the performances varied each night as the actors freely played at being animals and grotesque creatures. Stanislavsky had not yet conquered the basic problem of the actor's inspiration. Many of *The Blue Bird* performers were shocked and offended when Stanislavsky voiced his general disappointment; what did their director want from them?

THE BEGINNING OF THE SYSTEM

In the spring of 1909, Stanislavsky posted a notice at the MAT announcing that he was about to rehearse a new production in a way that no play had ever been created. His dramatic vehicle was to be Ivan Turgenev's *A Month in the Country,* a simple piece of psychological realism that was even less theatrical than any Chekhov play. Many of the younger MAT players responded enthusiastically. A few older members joined in the experiment as well.

Over a period of four months, the basic foundations of Stanislavsky's System were articulated and tested. Suler instructed the actors in yogic relaxation techniques, demonstrating the relationship between breath control and bodily tension. Other sessions in concentration showed how the actor could learn to focus his attention on objects and then in small and larger circles around the stage. To recreate the naive and direct artistic power of children or primitive people, performers played children's games and imitated animals. According to Suler, Relaxation, Concentration, and Naiveté were the initial steps in acquiring the Creative State of Mind. Together, Stanislavsky and Suler laid down these basic building blocks of the System.

In addition, each performer practiced "radiating his soul" as he sat at a table, signaling the subtextual thoughts of Turgenev's characters. Others attempted to "receive the arrows" of those intentions. Sometimes the actors could only use their eyes to communicate the dialogue and their hidden thoughts; other times they looked across the table, silently mouthing their lines. Their real feelings had to parallel those of the Turgenev characters. Large portions of the dialogue from *A Month in the Country* were cut from the text, forcing the actors to fill in with improvised speech. For the first time in the MAT's history, the essential creativity of the theatre had shifted away from the playwright and director to the side of the performer.

Several of the older actors broke down during the training. There was too much to keep in one's head. After watching one rehearsal, Nemirovich-Danchenko feared that *A Month in the Country* would certainly be a personal humiliation for Stanislavsky. But as undramatic and weak as the play was, the opening night finally proved to be an astounding victory for Stanislavsky's and Suler's methods. Even Nemirovich-Danchenko began to think that Stanislavsky had not been as crazy as he first appeared. Since it was not for the tastes of all actors, classes in the System, Nemirovich-Danchenko declared, were to be made an extracurricular part of the MAT's training.

Stanislavsky started to check for whatever theatrical and scientific literature might support his empirical investigations. Students and assistants with skills in foreign languages were sent off to libraries to uncover helpful sources. For some five years, Stanislavsky requested translations from French, Italian, English, and German texts. In the philosophical writings of Denis Diderot, for example, and the autobiographical accounts of such actors as Luigi Riccoboni, Talma, and La Clarion, Stanislavsky found material on some technical means of acting inspiration. Any field of learning held potential revelations. One important author, the French psychologist, Théodule-Armand Ribot, wrote in 1896 that to re-experience an emotion, one must first re-experience the emotion's imprint. By recalling the sensory atmosphere of a past activity, one can recapture the past emotion. Slowly, Stanislavsky began assembling the theoretical foundations of his System.

While taking a cure on the Isle of Capri in 1911, Stanislavsky rediscovered the spirit of the Commedia dell'arte as he watched the antics of travelling Italian street performers. Improvisation in performance, he saw, forces the actor to create before the audience's eyes. Without the yoke—or the guiding hand—of the playwright's scripted dialogue, the art of the stage (or the spectator's perception of it) becomes equated solely with the performer's skills. The feeling that the actor himself is the "creator" on the stage became a central feature for his evolving System. In Italy, Stanislavsky also began to study Hindu philosophy and yoga. Curiously, rather than making him more serious, this new knowledge enlivened him. On Capri's beaches, Stanislavsky could be seen playing games with children when he wasn't spontaneously performing comic monologues and tragic scenes from Symbolist dramas. He returned to Moscow in a healthy mood.

GORDON CRAIG'S "HAMLET"

Between 1909 and 1911, elaborate preparations for the Gordon Craig *Hamlet* production leeched much of Stanislavsky's energy. From the first days of the project, problems multiplied at a dizzying rate for both Stanislavsky and Suler. A firm believer in the notion that the performer should be an Übermarionette in the hands of director, Craig discounted the creative independence of actors and thought even less of the individual artistry of actresses. Trying to break out of his old Saxe-Meiningen directorial mold, Stanislavsky wanted to accommodate and understand Craig, as much as he could, for the sake of their innovative collaboration. But some aspects of this project were doomed from the beginning. Conflict and reversal followed the *Hamlet* venture at every turn.

Both Craig and Stanislavsky envisioned this same *Hamlet* as a grandiose and triumphant showcase for their respective theories and experiments. Each of them foresaw the production as a startling display of advanced theatrical technique: *Hamlet* as a spectacular model of the future theatre. Unfortunately, their conceptions clashed at each turn despite Stanislavsky's courtly attempts to mask over the artistic and personal disputes. A theatricalist, Craig conceived of *Hamlet* as an abstract monodrama with Hamlet visible on the stage in every scene. Huge movable screens, columns, stairways, and platforms illuminated with fantastic lighting and enormous shadows dwarfed Hamlet in a menacing world of mazes and traps, where the contorted characters were merely figments of Hamlet's imagination. Over the years of correspondence and meetings with his MAT hosts, Craig argued that the entire history of the theatre and mankind could be told through this production. Craig saw Hamlet as a superhuman visionary like Dionysus or Christ and hoped that Stanislavsky would cast himself in the part. Nemirovich-Danchenko vetoed the suggestion. Like others at the MAT, he felt Stanislavsky had few qualities as a tragedian. The thirty-six-year-old MAT favorite, Vasily Kachalov was given the lead.

For Stanislavsky, however, *Hamlet,* no matter how it unfolded in stylistic extremes, had to be intelligible on a primary level for his audience. Realist, Symbolist, Chekhovian, Naturalist, and fantasy elements found their way into the production. But in every case, Stanislavsky maintained a specific and actable line of direction. More and more aspects of his System appeared in acting as younger MAT members replaced ailing or disappointed veterans during the long rehearsal process. Kachalov and a few of the old guard actors took special sessions of exercises in the System. The result was a more powerful, understated interpretation of *Hamlet* than had ever been seen in Russia. So wrote the Moscow critics, including some who were naturally antagonistic to the MAT style. The finished production itself fared less well. When it was finally mounted in January 1912, Craig's monstrous flats and screens were too massive to slide across the stage. What might have been a milestone in blending System acting and modernist set design never fully materialized. Stanislavsky returned to the development of his System.

THE MAT'S FIRST STUDIO

To placate Nemirovich-Danchenko and other members of the MAT board, who started to grow less fond of the System training, Stanislavsky redirected his acting experiments to a separate and private arena, the First Studio. Formed in 1912, the First Studio consisted of fifteen or so young members and initiates of the MAT. Stanislavsky and Suler realized that only younger, less stage-experienced performers could follow their revolutionary training scheme. A natural teacher with a strong spiritual tendency, Suler believed more in transforming life than improving art. According to him, the theatre revealed the unspoken, hidden language between people. The new actor, who relies on truth and experience for his expression and inspiration, could expose—and therefore change—the everyday world of lies. The ordinary theatre was built on an artificial means of histrionics, or hysterical acting, that affects the nervous system of the spectator. Hysteria, according to Suler, was the result of one's refusal to feel deeply. System acting, built on a truthful and personal technique of expression, would create a direct communication from the actor's soul to that of the audience. The demand for minute detail in the System's acting was unrelated to any naturalistic ethos, Suler wrote in response to Stanislavsky's critics, but rather to show the audience everything in life, to hide nothing. The actor had to be trained to both feel and express all of his inner states fully.

In the spring of 1912, the First Studio officially began. Using his own money, Stanislavsky rented the top floor of the former Lux cinema building and paid the monthly salaries of the First Studio members. Although Suler led most of the sessions, there was an attempt to encourage the students to create their own exercises, scenic innovations, and theatrical visions. Stanislavsky frequently came to his laboratory, but his cold intellectual presence was often resented by the young actors. They secretly mocked his psychophysical demonstrations as soon as he left the Studio. More annoying was Stanislavsky's directorial attempts to instruct through imitation. And worse still was the old master's forgetfulness; time after time, Stanislavsky would complain about a student's work, not realizing that the pupil was merely following a previous day's command. On the other hand, Suler's warm and energetic personality—Gorky called him "a wise child"—gave the Studio its freshness and drive. It was only years later that the intense feasts of love and creativity in the Studio gave way to anarchy and chaos, where ferocious arguments broke out between those who believed in Affective Memory, as defined by Ribot, and those who championed Visualization (or Imagination) as sources for emotion.

Declaring that the First Studio needed its own communal "Pushkino," Stanislavsky sent the young members to a retreat near the Black Sea, where they constructed their own collective in the summer of 1912. Under Richard Boleslavsky's direction, they prepared their first production, *The Wreck of the Ship "Hope"*. Improvisations, exercises that began with animal imitations for characters, and Affective Memory work formed much of the rehearsal time. Boleslavsky invented exercises that embodied the rhythm and overall atmosphere (or "long distance mood") of the sea. Like the simple sets, each character and movement was stripped bare to uncover its psychological underpinnings. Every emotion found a clear and vivid expression. Stanislavsky himself encouraged them not to be afraid of overacting; it is always easier to take off, than add to a part. But the Studio's sense of depth and simplicity became their trademarks. In January 1913, *The Wreck* succeeded as a laboratory piece. Not only did Stanislavsky find praise for it, but the entire MAT Board was so impressed that they finally decided to fund the First Studio activities.

The First Studio's next presentation, *The Festival of Peace* by Hauptmann, received a less than glowing response. Some even thought that Evgeni Vakhtangov, the director and favorite pupil of Stanislavsky, had conducted a near fatal experiment in "out-Stanislavskying Stanislavsky." Staged in a tiny, almost claustrophobic theatre space,

Vakhtangov played upon *Festival*'s dark unbearable naturalist milieu. At close range, the Studio performers produced
authentic and pathetic emotional states that provoked a wave
of hysteria in its spectators. All agreed that it was an abuse
of the System and the trust of a sympathetic audience.

In the summer of 1914, Suler and Vakhtangov, with the
First Studio members, worked furiously on a full adaptation
of Charles Dickens' *The Cricket on the Hearth*. In some
ways it was intended as a correlative to the Hauptmann
piece. *Cricket* celebrated life and the human spirit. The First
Studio actors conscientiously built their own toy properties
and scenery. One of the Studio axioms was never to use
stage hands or technicians; the actors themselves were expected to create every aspect of a production. This not only
produced a fierce solidarity among the members, it also
brought them into a special relationship with their theatrical
props and tools.

Partly due to its spiritual opposition to the growing war
fever, but mostly because of the pure and personalized characterizations, *Cricket* was an immediate hit. In fact, its un-
equivocal success, especially in acting, forever established
Stanislavsky's System. Critics quickly declared the Studio's
performances superior to those of the MAT. The Studio's
long and unusual period of actor training also began to bear
fruit. When Vera Soloviova, for instance, had problems
crying on command in the role of Bertha, she used an
Affective Memory of her mother's death. Streams of tears
quickly followed. After six performances, other Affective
Memories were needed to create the powerful stimulus, but it

proved that Stanislavsky's technique could actually work.

One year later in 1916, the ailing Sulerzhitsky died, opening a huge personal and esthetic void in the First Studio's existence. Soloviova declared that Stanislavsky gave the First Studio members knowledge. He also donated space and money. But Suler gave his heart to the First Studio and in doing so introduced new life and a more human dimension into acting. Grief stricken, Stanislavsky appointed Vakhtangov as the artistic leader of the First Studio. Yet it was clear that Suler himself could never be replaced. More than twenty years later on his own death bed, Stanislavsky declared that a day did not go by when he did not think of his "dear Suler."

THE MAT IN THE REVOLUTIONARY EPOCH

When Bolshevik troops overran the center of Moscow in December 1917, they practically ignored the MAT building and the theatrical activities inside. Rifle fire outside was clearly audible during MAT productions that month. But inside performances continued uninterrupted. Aware that many Petrograd theatres had already been requisitioned for use by revolutionary councils, a worried Stanislavsky sent a brief letter to the ruling committee of the Moscow Soviet, requesting an immediate directive for his MAT and the First Studio. Just carry on, he was ordered. Those words encapsulated Stanislavsky's relationship with the Bolshevik government for a decade to come. Like the Kremlin walls, Gogol, and Tchaikovsky before him, Stanislavsky was part of a timeless and internationally-praised Russian culture. The Soviet respect for Stanislavsky's distaste of bald political propaganda on the MAT stage testified to the regime's early concern with creating a moderate image abroad and an esthetic continuity with Russia's past.

Long supported by the liberal element of the prerevolutionary bourgeoisie, however, the MAT now found itself in financial disarray and divided. The actors split into two warring groups: an anti-Bolshevik faction of the old guard that fled south and eventually emigrated to Prague; and the bulk of the company—some 150—who remained in Moscow with Stanislavsky and Nemirovich-Danchenko. Although the Revolution practically impoverished the Alexeyev clan along with the remaining aristocratic and landowning families in Russia, Stanislavsky continued his work for the New Russia. In fact, in many ways the post-revolutionary period proved to be a richer—if a more confused—time for the development of his System.

At age 55, Stanislavsky witnessed the beginnings of a national theatre-mania. While the MAT once prided itself on its immense popularity among Russia's upper classes and intelligentsia, the Revolution culturally enfranchised a nation of 100 million. Between 1918 and 1924, tens of thousands of teenagers and twenty-year-olds joined theatrical clubs and studios—or served in army agit-prop units—as the Bolsheviks consolidated power across Russia's west and south. Outdoor melodramas about Czarist oppression and the counterrevolutionaries' treachery; fairbooth satires that revealed Socialism's moral authority; and historic spectacles involving the participation of hundreds of thousands of performers and spectators evolved outside the traditional proscenium arches of Moscow. By 1923, when Lenin's New Economic Policy of limited capitalism started its second year, some forty different independent and State-supported studios and theatres advertised in Moscow's theatre guides and cultural newspapers. Even Stanislavsky's most promising pupils from the First Studio: Evgeni Vakhtangov, Michael Chekhov, and Valeri Smyshalayev had their own private studios and academies. The original Treplev in *The Seagull*, Meyerhold was suddenly glorified as the spiritual head of this grandiose upheaval that married modernist aesthetics with the social command of the Revolution.

Although Nemirovich-Danchenko had to attend to the problem of a new and frequently ill-mannered audience, especially in the early revolutionary years, the MAT managed to survive and prosper with government subsidies. Creatively, though, some members of the MAT felt stymied. The repertoire remained fixated on the MAT's past; between 1918 and 1923, only one new premiere was given, the ill-fated *Cain* by Lord Bryon, an unfortunate experiment in expressive movement. More disturbing still, once the lights dimmed in the MAT auditorium, it was as if the Revolution had never happened. Of course for many seated in the darkened theatre, this was its chief attraction. Just as the remounted productions brought back memories of a lost era, so the MAT itself grew to symbolize the Old Russia. One could escape the Soviet reality for a few hours at the MAT. It was a house of internal exile.

Stanislavsky long maintained that he would never become a mouthpiece for Soviet propaganda but, at the same time, he grew weary of the MAT's artistic complacency and passive social attitude. Nominally, Stanislavsky still retained the title of Artistic Director, yet his alienation from the MAT Board of Directors had increased. He barely spoke to Nemirovich-Danchenko. During rehearsals of the MAT adaptation of Dostoyevsky's *The Village Stepanchikovo* in the fall of 1917, Stanislavsky quarreled with Nemirovich-Danchenko's direction and single-layered interpretation of Stanislavsky's character. To everyone's surprise, Stanislavsky was immediately replaced. The humiliation of being fired in his own theatre a second time was another major turn in Stanislavsky's unsettled career. He swore that he would never again play a new role but only repeat past successes. In essence, Stanislavsky gave up performing as an actor. His artistic energies could now be refocused on the techniques and principles of actor training.

STANISLAVSKY'S ACTING CLASSES AT THE BOLSTOI OPERA

At the request of the Opera Section of the Bolstoi Theatre in 1918, Stanislavsky inaugurated a series of new lectures on his System and its relationship to musical performance. (A transcription of these talks can be found in David Magarshack's excellent *Stanislavsky on the Art of the Stage* [London, 1950].) Here the young students, who were for the most part already accomplished singers and opera performers, would be freshly indoctrinated in the themes and exercises of the First Studio's Creative State of Mind. For Stanislavsky too, the four-year experience allowed him to simplify and test his basic theories from Relaxation to Communication.

Before their classes with Stanislavsky, the student-singers gave little thought to their stage or character work beyond the perfection of their vocal qualities. When one baritone began to sing Valentine's aria from *Faust,* Stanislavsky interrupted him, declaring that the piece was unintelligible. The student balked. Was his diction poor? Stanislavsky told him no. In fact, it was quite good. The problem was in the meaning of the aria. "To whom are you singing?" Stanislavsky asked. The baffled student replied, to him, his teacher, the great Stanislavsky. The "Professor" reminded the student that he was singing to God; in the aria, Valentine is praying to God. The student was asked if he had ever prayed as a child. If so, to forget all about the class, his fellow singers, and to kneel and pray. Remembering the times of his childhood when he bowed before an icon, the baritone turned his back and kneeled. Beginning the song again, his rendition of Valentine's aria grew out of a deep emotional contact. To Stanislavsky and his class, the booming operatic tones gave way to a softer, more varied human voice: it was the true musical sound of a man appealing for divine inspiration. Stanislavsky proved that, like the actor, the opera singer, too, can make a deeper and more profound connection with his audience by delving beneath the stylistic, presentational conventions of the genre.

STANISLAVSKY'S FIRST PUBLIC
EXPLANATION OF THE SYSTEM

Despite the MAT's international popularity since its European tour, little was actually known or written about Stanislavsky's System before 1919. For many years Stanislavsky strictly forbade his students to even speak about it publicly. Leaks were uncommon because subservience to the Master was complete. The theatricalist director and writer Fyodor Komissarzhevsky wrote a polemical booklet in 1916, entitled *The Actor and Stanislavsky's Theory,* attacking what he thought were the foundations of the System: a dependence on naturalism; the creation of just two or three "sensations" (from his Affective Memory) for each performer over an entire evening; a vain attempt to throw out the actor's natural imagination and replacing it with a pseudo-scientific analysis of the "magic of acting." Without any firsthand knowledge of Stanislavsky's training technique or philosophy, Komissarzhevsky merely recorded prevailing gossip and clichés spread by First Studio detractors. Except for the accused themselves and a few theatre historians, almost no one paid much attention to Komissarzhevsky's diatribe.

After the Revolution, Michael Chekhov and Valeri Smyshalayev wrote short interpretations of the System for workers' publications and suffered Stanislavsky's wrath. Other members of the various studios of the MAT gave abbrievated workshops and lectures in the System, often with rushed and confusing results. (For the first time outside the MAT studios, actors complained about the idiocy of those exercises where they had to behave like insects and animals.) In 1919, Vakhtangov published a bitter attack on "Those Who Write of the Stanislavsky System." But, if anything, Vakhtangov's article was a veiled plea for the master himself to publish, if only in self-defense, his important accomplishments.

Finally in 1921, the first technical commentary by Stanislavsky on his System appeared in the journal anthology, *Teatralnaya Kultura*. It was entitled "Craft" and summarized the theoretical basis of his First Studio discoveries. According to Stanislavsky, three trends in acting were in existence in 1921: 1) Acting of Craft, 2) Acting of Image, and 3) Acting of Emotional Identification (or Experience).

Acting of Craft

The craftsman-actor has a limited means of expression based on stage clichés and his private storehouse of established responses to character types and texts. The principle strength or weakness of a stage feeling is normally indicated through the raising or lowering of the performer's voice. The craftsman-actor uses gestures and expressions to illustrate words rather than feelings. Movement on the stage frequently follows a preplanned pattern or an established pictorial compositon. Everything done on the stage is done with self-conscious care and therefore without real human emotion. To manufacture a feeling, the craftsman-actor will resort to physical tricks, forcing tears or laughter. Hyperventilation, for instance, would induce a state of anxiety. A follower of convention and instant results, the craftsman-actor takes great pride in his abilities to habitually mimic the work of greater craftsmen. The fact that his interpretation has been done before (or endlessly) is a source of satisfaction and comfort to him. Tricks, in other words, have become trademarked.

Acting of Image

By comparison, the image-actor may start work on a role by substituting events in the character's life with those in his own. Using his imagination and observations drawn from everyday life, he then adds different physical traits and psychological intentions to the character. He searches to find the character outside himself. After a period of trial and error, the image-actor has constructed his character. First he assimilates the character in rehearsal and then on stage demonstrates his results. Here, Stanislavsky claims, artistic creativity forms the core of the image-actor's interpretation, but such an actor refuses to actually create, or live, on stage. Although his physical conception of the character may be totally original, the image-actor behaves in an artifically rote manner. In more ways than he would like to think, the image-actor resembles the actor of craft, adding a bit more originality.

Acting of Emotional Identification (or Experience)

For Stanislavsky, only the third kind of actor, the one who emotionally experiences on stage, is fully creative. His acting preparations can be divided into three steps: 1) consciously creating the character's circumstances that are suggested by the playwright and director by learning and imagining all the details about the character's inner and external conditions; 2) unconsciously placing himself in the character's world, feeling his real feelings, through Affective Memory (the actor's remembered emotions); 3) embodying the physical and emotional character in an adjustment to the theatrical and directorial needs of the production. Unlike the image-actor, who uses his private memories or imagination *one time* to build the character in rehearsal, the performer of experience creates fully onstage and even changes during the life of the role. Rather than demonstrating his superb physical controls as the character, the experience-actor behaves as if everything onstage were happening to him *for the first time*.

The difference between these two actor-types is clear from the audience's response. In daily life, Stanislavsky wrote, people are normally only conscious of their activities some 10% of the time. On stage, the image-actor is 100% conscious of his characterization (which is to say, it is completely controlled). Watching this, the spectator knows internally that he is only seeing an imitation of an individual. The actor of experience, however, works with his unconscious powers just as people do in everyday life, creating something more humanly and artistically profound. Also, the actor of experience creates a natural and dynamic fusion of his true inner character with that of the playwright's. Stanislavsky claimed that an actor trained in his System may not be a better moving or sounding performer than a good image-actor. But the Stanislavsky performer has the ability to connect and identify with the spectator's unconsciousness in such a way as to leave an impression lasting far beyond that of the image-actor.

The vividness of everyday human expression often etches itself on our private memories in a way that most acting cannot. Watching the reality of two men argue and then fight under a street light on a deserted street at night or a young couple, desperate in their first love, seated in the corner of a cheap restaurant strike us in a different and more forceful way than viewing normal actors imitating the same activities on stage. This is because silent or unconscious thoughts manifest themselves with more immediacy in life. As spectators, we naturally perceive and record mentally the real behavior of people (which include conscious and unconscious activity) more deeply than the physical miming of actors— although the actors' imitation may give us a direct but short-lived pleasure.

By stimulating his unconsciousness to react directly to dramatic realities, or circumstances, the actor of experience achieves a psychological truthfulness that recreates for the audience the startling impact of real life. But to work on this daring esthetic plane, the actor must spend a great deal of time exercising his inner life, or "working on oneself." To do this, Stanislavsky formulated a somewhat revised First Studio program of Relaxation, Concentration, Affective Memory, Sense of Truth, Beauty, Rhythm, Feeling of Logic, Communication with an Audience, and Radiation. Although the recalling of the performer's feelings through

Affective Memory comprised the creative core of Stanislavsky's System in 1921, it was only the first of two steps. Once having accomplished the arousal of emotions called for in the text (repeated in rehearsal until they come naturally), then the actor has to make the character stageworthy by means of physical embodiment—voice, inflection, body image, and movement.

FIRST STUDIO EXERCISES (1911-23)

Although the First Studio was both a producing unit and theatre laboratory, an atmosphere of "exercise madness" permeated all the years of its existence. Literally hundreds of exercises were tried and either incorporated or discarded. Under Sulerzhitsky's leadership, a Bible-like tome rested on a wooden stand by the door of the studio. In the book, these individual exercises and more complicated acting études (group or improvisational work) were entered. Students were encouraged to write their commentaries on the work as well as invent and test out their own training techniques. During the First Studio's initial years, special days were set aside for this practice.

Truly a laboratory that functioned by trial and error, no single standardized curriculum of actor training was established during the years of the First Studio. The training changed constantly. Frequently the actors only practiced or "tested" one feature or aspect of the System on a given day. Before the First Studio's stage successes and the Revolution, everything was in flux; evolving and ever changing. Stanislavsky and Suler always viewed their work as experimental and imperfect. This was the primary reason there was so much hesitation about revealing the System either in print or in a set program. A premature definition or fixed regimen could lead, they felt, to a false and rigid program of actor training. And the two First Studio founders knew that their critics were ready to make such charges. Still, certain areas of System training developed over the years 1911 to 1923.

Relaxation, Concentration, and Naiveté were the essential and oldest features of Stanislavsky's notion of the Creative State of Mind. These formed the building blocks for the actor's "working on himself." Affective Memory, Communication, and Rhythm, although practiced in classroom exercises, were frequently associated with the private and individual process of "creating the role."

Sources for the exercises: *Michael Chekhov's articles on the Stanislavsky System in* Gorn #2-3 and 4 *(Moscow, 1919); Pavel Markov,* The First Studio *(Moscow, 1925); Michael Chekhov,* The Path of the Actor *(Moscow-Leningrad, 1928); materials given to Lee Strasberg during his 1934 Moscow trip; unpublished 1937 transcription of Michael Chekhov's lecture on First Studio exercises; transcriptions of Stanislavsky's 1918-22 lectures published in* On the Art of the Stage *(London, 1950); the anthology, L.Z. Sulerzhitsky,* Long and Short Stories *(Moscow, 1970); and interviews with First Studio member, Vera Soloviova, made by my students (1978-82).*

RELAXATION

The creative importance of a relaxed body was one of Stanislavsky's first major discoveries. The actor's greatest enemy is muscular tension, which limits his ability to feel as well as move. During the First Studio period, Stanislavsky believed that bodily tension could be released through isolation of the affected areas and also through breath control.

1. Lie down on the floor facing upwards. Tense your whole body briefly, then release all of the muscles on just your right side. For the next ten minutes, observe your body's reaction. Be aware of habitual tension creeping back into parts of your right side. Try to isolate these tense areas and relax them separately. Repeat the same exercise, focusing on the left side. Then repeat again, relaxing the whole body.

2. Sit down in a chair, allowing your arms, legs, and shoulders to relax completely. With your head and neck straight, raise your hands over your head and spread your fingers wide apart. Then close them into a fist and open them again. Begin to match the spreading and closing of your fingers with your breathing. Open your fist, one finger at a time, as you inhale. Your breathing and hand rhythms must blend harmoniously with one another.

3. Complicate the above exercise by opening only two fingers as you inhale. Then create a new rhythm with three fingers. Add music. Following these sound rhythms will alter your breathing and hand rhythms again.

4. Pick up various small objects from the floor—a pencil,

notebook, or ring. Observe which muscle units are needed and repeat the activity, using the least amount of energy.

CONCENTRATION

The development of the actor's ability to focus or concentrate on a single sensation or object is the first step necessary in producing the Creative State of Mind. By concentrating on this object, the actor learns to make himself interested in it. This, in turn, takes his attention away from the audience, bringing him directly and unerringly into the stage reality.

5. Without looking, count the change in your pockets.

6. Mentally compute a mathematical problem.

7. Carefully study the physical make up of your fingers. Concentrate on the smallest details that separate your fingers from everyone else's. Look at the nails, the joints, the hair, the texture of the skin, each finger's length and circumference. Try to invest each physical characteristic with a past. For instance, a scar might have come from a childhood accident.

8. Concentrate on the drawing of simple figures of squares, circles, triangles.

9. Study the pattern on some wallpaper, a picture, or a carpet.

10. Study the chandelier or the carpet for ten or fifteen minutes. Discover something extraordinary about it. Describe it.

11. Take in as many details as possible from your partners clothing. Be able to describe them.

12. Listen to a sound. Single out and trace only one sound out of a mass of many.

13. Concentrate mentally on some musical phrase while listening to choral singing or piano playing.

14. Begin several activities: look at magazine pictures, listen to music, dance, solve a mathematical problem, play a game. Move quickly from one activity to another. In each segment, concentrate completely on the first before you pass onto the next.

15. Try to silently suggest a definite idea to someone.

16. Read from a book as your partner does the same. Transfer your attentions from your book to your partner and then back to the book.

Exercises in Divided Attention

Onstage, actors are placed in situations where they must react to or perform several activities simultane-

ously. Exercises in Divided Attention both test the ac-tor's ability to concentrate in the midst of constant dis-traction and train him to perform one mental activity while executing a second physical task.

17.   Completely absorb yourself in a book. Concentrate on it for meaning and understanding. While other actors attempt to distract you, by telling stories, singing, making fun of you, continue to read until you no longer notice them.

18.   Compute the following equation 182 x 24 as others ask you questions.

19.   Concentrate on finding the solution to a difficult prob-lem. Let several persons ask you questions persis-tently and simultaneously. Solve your problem while answering the others.

CREATIVE CIRCLE

An exercise concept in increasing the powers of Con-centration, the Creative Circle trains the actor to be-come acutely aware of his immediate surroundings. He must concentrate only within the imaginary circle around him. The Circle can grow in size from a three-foot circumference around the actor's body to an area encompassing the entire stage.

20. Concentrate on a single point that is close to you. The corner of a table, for example. Study it. Allow your body to relax. Whenever you feel your mind wavering, return to the same fixed point.

21. Do the same as above only concentrate on a point that is a middle distance from you. Then concentrate on another point that is far away.

22. Focus all your thoughts on a knife that you are holding. Its purpose is to murder your rival. First concentrate on your action by examining the knife. Look at it closely. Test the blade. Is it sharp enough, long enough? How is the handle weighted, constructed? Think clearly: Can the knife accomplish the deed? Is it strong enough to pierce a human heart?

23. Widen your circle of thought to the knife's object: your rival. Instead of fixing your thoughts on his evil deeds, think of the good times you both shared: your childhood games, the time he saved your life. Remember the happy details. Let these images build in your mind. But the sharpness of the blade reminds you of your mission, to kill him, and your reasons for doing it. You remember the torment of his betrayal, the lies and deceits. Your circle now covers the knife, your future action, and your whole relationship with your rival.

24. Walk around the room, creating a small and then a

large circle. You must have the ability to absorb all the activity and objects in your circle and hold it in your concentration. Be aware of the other actors who enter into your circle as they inscribe their own personal ones. Each actor brings a different size circle onstage. Attempt to feel the strength and width of your partner's circles.

NAIVETÉ

An inherent human quality, Naiveté is usually lost after childhood. It is the ability and desire to believe fully and truthfully in the unseen. To enter into a play's imaginary circumstances, the actor must relearn and develop his childlike powers to completely believe in invisible stimuli.

25. You are a child in a playground. Instead of shouting or worrying about physical imitations, follow a child's logic and his ability to abruptly concentrate on any interesting activity.

26. Ask your partner for a pencil while pretending to carry one of the following: a revolver, razor, dagger, or snake. Observe how your relationship is transformed.

27. Walk across the floor as though it were a puddle or burning hot sand.

28. Assume a series of the most grotesque and laughter-provoking postures. Believe that these are necessary for your personal happiness.

29. Invent some unusual ritual and perform it with utmost seriousness.

30. *The Circus:* observing the ways and habits of animals, you must present yourself as a circus animal. (This can be the key to finding a stage character. For instance, the character of an old Jewish woman can begin with imitating an old nag; a coquette, a young colt.)

31. Try to discover beauty everywhere: in every thought, position, picture, and posture.

IMAGINATION

Nearly all acting is the result of the performer's ability to imagine. Imagination for the First Studio's members, however, took on a special, more intensive meaning. They related it to Naiveté and Affective Memory. In developing their imaginations through game-like exercises, the First Studio actors hoped to overcome the MAT's reputation for solemn, thickly layered acting, punctuated with long, heavy pauses. The quick, spontaneous "leaps of the imagination" in children's mental and physical activities more closely reflected how the First Studio actors wanted to be per-ceived onstage. Only training in Naiveté and Imagina-tion could make their repeated performances seem as if they were happening "for the first time."

32. Find the resemblances between objects and specific persons. Find resemblances between selected persons and animals.

33. Listen to different pieces of music and transform them into fantastic images with your body.

34. After your partner gives you a word, improvise on it. Then add qualities of sorrow, joy, and mystery.

35. Make natural or unidentifiable noises while others sit with their backs turned to you. 1) They must sponta-neously visualize pictures that correspond to the sounds. 2) Repeat the exercise using a different mood or quality. 3) Repeat the sounds once more but this time the listeners have set images in mind beforehand. They then must justify the meaning of your noises as they apply to their images.

36. Remember a street or path that you walk past daily. Break it into separate sections. Create a story that links each of the sections of the street.

37. Pretend that you are a clairvoyant and arrange a séance.

38. Eat a bowl of soup as if a great tragedy had just befall-

en you, the death of your child, for instance. Now eat the soup as if you had won a lottery.

39. Your group is seated at table. Someone utters a word. Using the first image that comes to mind, the next person conveys it with a sound or subtle gesture.

========================

AFFECTIVE MEMORY

Later divided into Sense Memory and Emotional Recall, Affective Memory is the practice of producing controlled sensations and emotional reactions in the actor. Recalling the sensory details of a simple memory, like the feeling of snow against his face, for instance, the actor learns to re-experience the sensation onstage. More complicated emotions, like love and fear, are stimulated through vivid memories from the actor's own life. As much as two hours could be necessary to stimulate an Emotional Recall in a first session. Often, this can be reduced to one minute after several months of practice.

40. Remember the moments in your life when you most strongly felt anger, love, suffering, joy, hatred, surprise, sadness, or fear.

41. Now reconstruct in your mind the detailed circumstances and factors (sense stimuli) that caused those emotions in you. Begin to slowly feel the smallest of

the sensory details that you can recall from memory.

42. Having recreated an emotion, now work on another memory to quickly replace it with another emotion. Practice until you can go from one emotion to three other ones over a fifteen minute period.

Études [or Directed Improvisations] Used to Inspire Affective Memory

43. In your house, your father is dangerously ill. While waiting for a physician to come, guests arrive and have to be entertained.

44. A poor relative in need of money comes into your house and discovers guests there.

45. Just before a concert a pianist becomes agitated. Her friends attempt to quiet her down.

46. Although your wife is very ill at home, you, a doctor, must leave to see another patient somewhere else.

47. You meet a man who you thought disappeared many years ago.

48. While a husband and wife are quarrelling, guests arrive at their home.

49. Relatives see off someone who is going on a long voyage.

50. At an art exhibition, a crowd of people looks over the paintings, voices their feelings, scans each other's clothing, and gossips.

COMMUNICATION

To go beyond the playwright's words, an actor must learn to deliver a deeper, living message to the audience. This cannot be accomplished through a direct contact with the spectator. Instead, the actor transfers specific thoughts, not words, to his partner, which then affects the audience. Facial expression, movement, and vocal tone are the normal means of creating a character interaction outside the overt meanings of the dialogue. Radiation of Prana rays, directly from the actor's being, however, can be the most intense form of Communication.

51. Using the question, "What time is it?" communicate to your partner the following thoughts: 1) Am I late? 2) Why are you so late? 3) Why don't you leave? 4) My God, this is boring! 5) Please tell me the time.

Prana Exercises

Prana is a Sanskrit word referring to the waves of a universal life force. Stanislavsky and Suler believed that invisible rays of Prana could be produced in the

hands, finger tips, and eyes of the performer. Coming
from the actors' souls, ultimately they could be felt in
the audience.

52. From your fingertips spread Prana rays out to God, to
    the sky, to your partner.

53. Stretch your hands out and emit rays from the tips of
    your fingers to only one "receiver" in a row of class-
    mates. All of the students should be seated with their
    backs to you. Although all of them have their palms
    behind their backs ready to receive your rays, only the
    "receiver" should actually feel your Prana.

Études in Communication

54. In the reading room of a library, you silently attempt to
    signal a friend to meet you outside.

55. You are a fisherman who has waited silently all morn-
    ing for a bite. You try to quiet a woman who is
    singing loudly in an approaching boat.

56. As a paralyzed person unable to speak, you must
    somehow communicate your feelings to your doctor or
    answer his questions.

RHYTHM

All human activity follows some rhythmic pattern, which can be felt by the actor and expressed physically. Every stage movement should be conceived in Rhythm. Also, each character has a private Rhythm. Finding the character's Rhythm is an essential key to discovering his personality. According to Stanislavsky, Romeo and Juliet, for instance, will never come together because their hearts beat to different rhythms, not because of any family disputes.

57. Find the correct rhythm for moving furniture, making the bed, turning the pages of a book, putting your books away.

58. Dress under the following time constraints, as if you had: 1) five hours before a performance, 2) one hour, and 3) five minutes. Now recreate the three rhythms of dressing without thinking of the time constraints.

59. Discover your character's favorite song. Convert it into rhythmic activity. This will bring you into his world and personality.

60. Give your character three completely different rhythms. See how this transforms his personality and interactions with other characters.

CHAPTER THREE

EVGENI VAKHTANGOV'S REFORMULA-
TIONS OF THE SYSTEM

Oy, Vakhtangov! Vakhtangov, Vakhtangov, Vakhtangov,
Vakhtangov!

> A student of Vakhtangov's 1921 Studio,
> slapping her face from side to side, in
> reply to the author's question, "What was
> it like to work with Vakhtangov?" 1979.

EARLY YEARS AND DEVELOPMENT

Born in 1883 into the family of a wealthy Armenian tobacco merchant, Evgeni Vakhtangov suffered greatly as a
child from emotional neglect and a lack of love. From the
earliest age he found himself driven into the fantasy worlds
of dance, music, and theatre. Make-believe became his total
universe. Unlike Stanislavsky, who was also a skillful
businessman, or the itinerant jack-of-all-trades Sulerzhitsky,
for whom the performing arts were merely another spiritual
vehicle, Vakhtangov lived, thought, and dreamed only the-

atre. His legendary energy and passion, his inexhaustible creativity, carried him deeper and deeper into a quest for the most perfect theatrical presentations. It finally cost him his health and then his life.

By the age of eighteen, Vakhtangov was already staging amateur, but highly praised versions of such plays as Anton Chekhov's comedies, *The Bear* and *The Marriage Proposal.* Every production detail, from lighting design to intensive biographical studies of the playwrights, was rigorously researched by Vakhtangov. No aspect of theatre escaped his attention or was too trivial for study. In a university production of Sergei Nedolin's *Zinochka,* for example, Vakhtangov assembled over forty pages of preparatory notes on the characters and the play's presentation. Clearly, Vakhtangov's devotion and skills were far beyond amateur, and many newspaper reviewers extolled his undertakings. Some critics even compared his directorial work favorably with that of the MAT.

In 1904, Vakhtangov entered Moscow University's Department of Jurisprudence, ostensibly to pursue a career in law. But more of his time was spent at local theatres and with the student theatrical societies which he headed. By the summer of 1909, one year shy of his law degree and after acting and directing in a dozen or so performances, Vakhtangov made his final break with the university and his family's wishes. He dropped out of law school in order to study acting seriously at the progressive Adashev School of Drama. It was here that Sulerzhitsky taught the rudiments of the System, in a special arrangement to separate Stanislavsky's acting experiments from his other work at the MAT. Suler quickly recognized Vakhtangov's craft and talent. At the end of 1909, he invited Vakhtangov to assist him on a production of Maeterlinck's *Blue Bird* in Paris. Completing the Adashev curriculum in 1911, Vakhtangov was immediately engaged by the MAT, playing the Gypsy in Lev Tolstoy's *The Living Corpse,* the Player-Queen in the Gordon Craig *Hamlet,* and other minor roles. Suler also began to groom the twenty-nine-year-old Vakhtangov as a teacher of the System. And in October 1912, they officially founded the First Studio of the MAT.

VAKHTANGOV IN THE FIRST STUDIO

Vakhtangov's first directorial assignment for the First Studio, the mounting of Gerhart Hauptmann's *The Festival of Peace,* caused enormous controversy. In fact, the MAT board cancelled all public performances of it in November 1913. Fanatically following Stanislavsky and Suler's principles, Vakhtangov hoped his direction in *The Festival of Peace* would penetrate the normal acting barriers of his young performers, producing true and dynamic feelings that would arouse and shock the First Studio spectators. He succeeded only too well. Moments of quiet psychological intensity were suddenly interrupted by emotional outbursts that appeared more real than theatrical. The extreme contrasts of acted emotions onstage and the performers' physical proximity to the spectators in the confined studio space whipped many in the audience into hysterical fits of weeping. Vakhtangov knew how to draw out the psychological truths from his performers, but as a director, many MAT members felt, he had abused Stanislavsky's teachings and his own genius by manipulating the spectator's responses. Despite the unrealistic backdrops, Vakhtangov had created a hyper-realism in the acting.

One month later, Vakhtangov went outside the MAT to establish his own amateur group, the Drama Studio, the first of many independent theatre groups that he would found or direct up until his death. The young students' enthusiasm and desire to work proved seductive. Beyond the MAT's censuring board Vakhtangov hoped he could stage his own experiments. But their first production, Boris Zaitzev's *Lanin's Country Estate,* was an embarrassment. Opening in March 1914, the students tried to imitate the MAT's Chekhovian productions with offstage sounds and even lilac scents. Although they attempted to create truthful emotions, the actors' amateurish characterizations and lack of scenic composition in movement and speech bored the Drama Studio's audiences. From this Vakhtangov learned a valuable lesson: acting must always have both depth and form.

In the summer of 1914 the three-year-old First Studio of MAT began rehearsing in earnest. With war approaching in the West, Suler immersed First Studio members in an adaptation of Charles Dickens' *Cricket on the Hearth.* Playing the part of the villainous Tackleton with the clacking movements of a mechanical toy, Vakhtangov received accolades from all the critics on opening night, November 24th, 1914. Vakhtangov was quickly viewed as the the First Studio's leading actor, much to the dismay of his colleague Michael Chekhov.

During the First Studio's summer tour of the Russian provinces in 1915, Chekhov and Vakhtangov, now roommates as well as rivals, quarreled frequently about every petty matter. But their closeness also lead to discoveries about acting. Chekhov remembered one such occasion when the two of them were playing billiards. Each unable to sink even one pool ball in the pocket, they grew frustrated and agreed to call it a night. Suddenly, Vakhtangov announced, "Watch this!" Changing his entire physical stance and attitude, Vakhtangov sank ball after ball while Chekhov watched in amazement. After Vakhtangov finally missed a shot, a startled Chekhov asked how such prowess was possible. Vakhtangov replied that he decided to imagine that he was the greatest pool player ever, taking on his posture, movements, and way of thinking. Vakhtangov explained that he himself could never play billiards as brilliantly as his character.

In December 1915, Vakhtangov presented his first successful MAT production, Henning Berger's *The Deluge*. Set in the Rocky Mountains of the American West, *The Deluge* begins with a group of odious American businessmen and workers arguing in a saloon. At the conclusion of the First Act, they discover that the tavern is about to be washed away in a rapidly advancing flood. During the Second Act, as their lives are about to come to an end, all their behavior changes: they discover their need and love for one another. At the end of the act, it is announced that the direction of the flood has shifted. Their lives are saved. In the Third Act, they have returned to their hateful ways. In *The Deluge,* Vakhtangov developed rhythm and tempo for each of the characters' behavior. For instance, to establish a frenzied American tempo, Vakhtangov had a minor character do the following in the background: rush into the saloon; order and gulp down in rapid succession soup, a whole chicken, and dessert; pay the bill and leave, all in one swift action. While maintaining a pronounced rhythmic sense and mood, Vakhtangov helped create in his actors a sharply felt individuality and humanity for each of the play's characters. Even the most evil or grotesque among the characters revealed a gentle or loving core. The Tolstoyan message, a belief that men are wolves who can be purified through love or the approach of death, was never better presented.

After Suler's death in 1916, Stanislavsky handed Vakhtangov, Suler's chosen heir, the reigns of the First Studio. But not everyone at the MAT approved this selection. Vakhtangov was known for his hot temper and uncompromising personality. Sometimes the smallest infraction of rules by Studio members, like forgetting to clean the floors at the end of a rehearsal session, left Vakhtangov in a rage. In addition, Vakhtangov was gravely ill. Yet his psychological reaction to his various ailments (tuberculosis and stomach cancer), rather than depressing or slowing him down, pushed him to increase his physical activity.

From 1917 to 1922, roughly the period of the Russian Revolution and Civil War, Vakhtangov fought desperately against premature death. Going from studio to studio—

sometimes as many as six or eight in an evening—Vakhtangov attempted to improve upon Stanislavsky's System in the shortest possible time. He directed, taught, and lectured at Soviet, independent, and amateur schools and studios, soothing his stomach pains with an ubiquitous glass of water, foaming with bicarbonate of soda. Vakhtangov's students and young performers knew that each inspiring lesson or étude could be his last. And unlike his MAT colleagues, Vakhtangov welcomed the Bolshevik Revolution and thrived on the energy it inspired. In 1918, he staged Ibsen's *Rosmersholm* and Maeterlinck's *Miracle of Saint Anthony* before new revolutionary audiences. His idea of the "festival spirit" in the theatre began to emerge in these productions. The theatre, he said, exists to celebrate the joy of life. The same dour characters and dialogues of humanistic realism that once brought tears to the old MAT audiences, now produced laughter and seemed anachronistic.

VAKHTANGOV'S NEW ACTING THEORIES

Although Vakhtangov would constantly defend Stanislavsky's theories in public, by the time of the Revolution in 1918, Vakhtangov's private teachings began to depart from the First Studio tradition. That the theatre was different from life and required a special means of external expression all its own was not exactly a revelation. The Symbolists had proclaimed the same idea since the turn-of-the-century. Essentially, Vakhtangov felt that the System inhibited the work of the actor. Like many of the new Soviet directors, Vakh-

tangov wanted to take the theatre far away from veri-
similitude, or everyday reality. But with Stanislavsky he
agreed that acting without an emotional or human basis could
never make a true (or subconscious) contact with the spectator. For many, Vakhtangov's concept constituted a
theatrical paradox: the creation of an acting technique that
was both outwardly stylized and internally realistic. Working feverishly over the final three years of his life, Vakhtangov was determined to prove his thesis with results.

Relaxation and Concentration

In 1919, Vakhtangov summarized his discoveries in a series of eight lectures. His agreement with Stanislavsky
showed strongly in the first two lectures on Relaxation and
Concentration, although Vakhtangov's versions gave somewhat different reasons for their acting importance. Stanislavsky maintained that muscular tension prevented the performer from executing small, detailed gestures. Vakhtangov
felt the opposite: tension (both physical and psychological)
encouraged the actor to engage in unmotivated and nervous
displacement activities on stage, such as touching his face or
hair, tapping a cigarette case, playing with his belt, and so
forth. This lack of physical control was a bane to both the
actor and director. Relaxation, therefore, is related to one's
physical confidence and artistic feeling for theatrical form.
Tension causes superfluous movements—a great enemy for
precise and stylized acting.

Like his mentor, Vakhtangov thought that Relaxation and Concentration were linked. But, typically, Vakhtangov placed a much greater emphasis on their use in performance. Every moment an actor is onstage, he must have an Object of Attention. These objects can be material, like an address book on a table or a partner's necklace, or invisible, like a crashing sound in another room, a personal memory, or a scent. Objects of Attention onstage naturally engage the actor's awareness as they would in life. Waiting in a strange room for more than a few minutes, a person will often look for an Object of Attention to command his interest or simply to ward off boredom. He picks up a magazine, looks at a painting on a wall, daydreams, smokes a cigarette, and so forth because his mind and senses want to focus on an activity. Although a performer can use many different kinds of Objects of Attention in a single scene, only one can be the subject at any given moment. According to Vakhtangov, this use of Concentration has a double benefit: it quickly guides the actor past the disturbing gaze of the audience into the more immediate realm of the stage, while at the same time the character's engagement enhances the audience's own interest and attention.

Faith, Naiveté, and Justification

Vakhtangov's third lecture, "Faith, Naiveté, and Justification," established his standing as a radical reformer of the Stanislavsky System. While Stanislavsky saw the actor's identification with the character in the Given Circumstances

—through parallels, correspondences, and substitutions—as the core of his early teachings, Vakhtangov sought a more immediate, and creative approach for the performer's interior work. He called this Justification, a technique that takes into account the actual thought processes of the actor. According to Vakhtangov, an artist can create only when he has faith in the importance of his creation. Alcohol fools the brain's censoring apparatus. Creative energy that is reserved for meaningful tasks can then be released. Yet an actor must believe in the significance of what is happening every second on the stage, not only when he feels inspired or is a bit drunk. Vakhtangov's solution was through Justification. To create a constant faith or naive belief in the importance and truth of a production, an actor must justify his particular presence on stage and the reality of each moment occurring in the theatre.

At the beginning of any project, an actor must ask himself the following basic questions: "Why am I in the theatre?" "Why am I in this group?" "Why am I in this play?" "Why am I playing this part?" In every instance, the actor must have a strong personal motive, or Justification. The answers, however, do not have to be either logical or related to the script. They need only appeal to the performer's rationale or inner need. For example, a performer can have a small walk-on part and justify his work by pretending that his role is crucial to the play's intelligibility or that a leading critic, sitting in the audience, who was once a spear carrier himself, will take notice of this actor's performance and single him out for a glowing review. More than anything, the individual mind must be convinced that the actor's work is significant.

To carry the process further, Vakhtangov believed that every gesture, every word, every nuance must be justified. If the director asks a performer to freeze at a certain place in the production, it is not enough to just stop his movement. The performer must justify the arrested pose to himself. He can pretend, for instance, that he is listening to the sounds of a burglar in the next room, waiting for a photographer to take his picture, or holding a dance partner while a record is being changed. A Justification that engages the artistic mind creates a dynamic inner life and reduces tension, since it can also function as an object of acting attention. The fundamental idea of Justification is to keep the actor's mind active and alert.

Stanislavsky and others were concerned with the notion of Justification. However, Vakhtangov's idea contained a surprising innovation from theirs: the performer's Justification could be unrelated to the circumstances of the play or character. Justification is the actor's secret. A performer who is directed to pace the stage and think of avenging his father's death, for example, may not be stimulated by the director's suggestion and find no inner reality in the action. But he could pretend to himself that the purpose of his pacing is to find a weak floorboard in order to fall through the stage and sue the theatre's management! The strength of the actor's fanatsy or Justification, no matter how ludicrous or unrelated to the given direction, could lead the actor into a more convincing and concrete sense of reality. Justification allows the performer to create a strong private reality in all types of productions, from the stylized abstract to the most traditionally realistic.

The Circle of Attention

The fourth lecture, entitled "The Circle of Attention," integrated the ideas of the first three. Using the image of a circle, or the circular area lighted by an electric bulb, Vakhtangov spoke of the "charged" field that surrounds the actor. This is the space where the actor focuses his concentration. Narrow at first and gradually expanding, the Circle of Attention schools the actor in observation and attention. Starting with his hands and a small object, the performer slowly widens his field of concentration and justifies his activities until he becomes aware of the entire stage. Stanislavsky also taught this concept, but Vakhtangov emphasized the actual use of the actor's hands to manipulate imaginary objects in the Circle. The preference for imaginary over real physical objects in this exercise, as well as others created by Vakhtangov, was another departure from Stanislavsky's teachings.

The Task

The elements of The Task, or what we might call the Action, was the subject of the fifth lecture. Here Vakhtangov trisects stage action into: 1) the Goal (why the actor has come on the stage); 2) the Desire (what the actor wants); and 3) the Adjustment (what the actor must do, based on the circumstances of the play or the direction). For example, the actor's Goal is to quiet an hysterical person. His Desire is to shake and slap the hysteric. However, the actor is directed not to touch him. One truthful Adjustment would be for the actor to feel pity and cry out of helplessness towards the hysterical character.

A common criticism of the Stanislavsky System, the precedence of the actor's private truth over the director's needs, was solved by Vakhtangov's idea of Adjustment. Both performer and director, Vakhtangov understood that MAT actors often found their director's blocking a severe handicap to their creative freedom. If, for example, a director requested a "hollow laugh" in the middle of Hamlet's soliloquy "To be or not to be," but the actor did not feel its "truth," an Adjustment (a new personal Justification) could be secretly added by the actor: Hamlet attempts to laugh at his situation to avoid feeling the fear of suicide.

Affective Memory

In the sixth lecture, "Affective Memory," Vakhtangov attacked the problem of "acted emotion." The performer cannot simply will his emotions automatically. They must be the product of real psychological stimuli. And when genuine emotions are aroused, they cannot be easily controlled. Sometimes their residue effects last for hours and can carry over into other scenes. Yet onstage, an actor may be asked to transform his feelings from grief to joy in the space of a few minutes as the production's scenes and acts change.

Therefore, actors must use, what Vakhtangov called, "remembered emotions."

These stage feelings, or Affective Memory, differ from living (or everyday) emotions. They are generated from the performer's emotional background and must be carefully adjusted to accommodate a production's specific needs. If an actor must suddenly feel the terror of death, for example, he can choose to psychologically recreate the Sense Memory of nearly drowning as a child or the more immediate shock of being told that the mushrooms he has just eaten may be poisonous, or whatever terrifying situation that can powerfully fill him with the emotions called for in the scene. Using his five senses, the actor can mentally relive these experiences and then adjust their intensity (or physicality) until they parallel the character's feeling of terror. Vakhtangov believed that the more an actor exercised his own Affective Memories, through constant recollection, the more quickly feelings would return to him and greater use could be made of them in his work. But Affective Memories, especially powerful ones, can be difficult to control and are not needed every moment in a character's stage life. Vakhtangov estimated, for example, that in any given Shakespearean play, an actor would need only a total of five minutes of them.

Tempos

In the seventh lecture, Vakhtangov discussed Tempos, or levels of energy, used to establish character reactions to shifting environments and circumstances. A man at a railroad cafe, for example, changes his Tempo of eating at the announcement of his train's departure or delay. His pace naturally quickens or slows according to the external circumstances. Each person and situation has its own special Tempo or rhythm. These change rapidly in a production, and the performer must be able to adjust to them quickly. As Vakhtangov later wrote, "Every person, every nationality, every occupation has its rhythm. To perceive the rhythm of the character means to understand the role. To find the rhythm of a play is to discover the key to its presentation."

Communication

Vakhtangov's final lecture dealt with Communication. Just as someone implicitly knows when a speaker is in command of his subject, an audience instantly intuits an actor's believability and enjoyment of his role. Ultimately, the source of Communication is the development and maintenance of "interest," profound interest or fascination, in the character, a partner's choices, the play, the audience, even in the atmosphere of boredom on the stage (if that is the director's choice). Spectators will only be moved, psychologically, to the extent that the actor moves them. In order to most fully communicate dramatic reality, the performer must first master actual realities on stage. For example, if his partner is required to cry in a scene, but fails to do so, the actor should never pretend that the other character has cried, but deal with the moment that has just happened. He should make an adjustment within his own acting. In life, this happens frequently. If at a funeral parlor you discover that none of the deceased's family is in mourning or crying, you naturally adjust yourself to their mood. The actor's job is not to carry out the preconceived plan of the director but, to communicate the character's immediate reality to the audience.

VAKHTANGOV'S FINAL PRODUCTIONS

In 1921, Vakhtangov's independent Studio was incorporated into the MAT as the Third Studio. Stanislavsky and the others were anxious to follow the result of Vakhtangov's theoretical teachings. Two productions (in several variations) were presented there during its first year: Anton Chekhov's short farce *The Wedding* and Maurice Maeterlinck's symbolic *Miracle of St. Anthony*. In addition, Vakhtangov directed Michael Chekhov in a First Studio production of August Strindberg's Hamlet-like *Erik XIV*. All three productions shared stylistic features of the grotesque, coarsely blending comedy and tragedy with horror. Every gesture and movement, every tone and glance and attitude were justified by the actors, which gave the performances a deeper personal dimension. To render a personal truth in a poetic phrase, an actor would have to find an equivalent situation in his own life where he spoke in such an elevated manner: for instance, delivering a funeral oration, making a sentimental toast, proposing marriage, or learning an archaic language. Each odd movement had to have an internal logic. Vakhtangov's actors were made to think as well as feel.

August Strindberg's "Erik XIV"

In *Erik XIV,* Vakhtangov experimented with a radical mise-en-scène. Just as the play could be made to turn on the contrasts of life and death, royalty and peasantry, duty and happiness, loyalty and deceit, so each and every theatrical detail was mirrored in striking and opposing effects. Sets, costumes, every visual element on stage appeared only in shocks of black and white, at acute and obtuse expressionistic angles. An upward flick of the wrist of one actor would be visually complemented by the downward tilt of the head of another performer. Sounds and movements trailed off, being masked, refuted, contradicted, and magically replaced. The young revolutionary audiences of Soviet Russia, Vakhtangov believed, were no longer interested in traditional plot construction or elegant character development. Only when bored did anyone consider those things. The ideal scenic moment—when performed with perfect artistic composition, control, and confidence—could communicate everything in an instant. A theatrical event could be seen as a series of paintings come alive. After all, Vakhtangov thought, on the street corners of Moscow, where automobiles with miniature red flags speed past blind beggars and handholding lovers, no continuity of plot or character is called for. It's when things seem phony or "staged" that a spectator will question their truthfulness.

Erik XIV, like all of Vakhtangov's later productions, left audiences excited and thrilled. Yet Vakhtangov differed from Meyerhold, Tairov, and the other avant-garde Soviet directors in his attitude toward actors. To begin with, actors who made their own character discoveries and choices performed in a completely different way than those who were placed and blocked on the stage like puppets, moving and speaking at the command or in imitation of their directors. In the MAT tradition, Vakhtangov wanted actors who were creators themselves. No matter how grotesque or modernist his productions looked, Vakhtangov never abandoned the importance of the actor's inner life. He asked that each performer start with a strong identification with his role: the substitution of personal or imaginary events in place of the character's. Secondly, that the actors privately justified the director's blocking needs and staging demands.

The Habima Players

In 1918, a group of young Jewish actors approached Stanislavsky for training and help in forming a new company, the Habima. The Revolution had already liberated millions of Jews from the oppressive Czarist edicts that limited where they could live and how they could make their living. Hundreds of thousands of Jews migrated east from the western Pale of Settlement to Moscow and other large cities in Russia's interior. For the first time in a generation, theatre for Jewish audiences, once strictly forbidden, was now possible. Linguistically, Moscow's Jews were divided into primarily Yiddish-speakers from the west and already assimilated native Russian-speakers. The Habima Players decided to perform in modern Hebrew, a new language that was being reinvented in Palestine from ancient Biblical sources. Although many Jews could read religious Hebrew texts and prayed in the language, few understood it as a spoken language. For the Habima, the making of Hebrew-language productions was a revolutionary statement. In doing so, they attempted to maintain their Jewish identity while participating in the Bolshevik social upheaval.

Since his productions of *Uriel Acosta* and *The Merchant of Venice,* Stanislavsky had been fascinated with Jewish culture and the "Jewish problem." But Stanislavsky had little time for this devoted troupe of amateurs. He suggested that they approach Vakhtangov, who, as an Armenian, was also a member of an oppressed minority. Besides preparing for his own Third Studio at this time, Vakhtangov also headed or taught at the MAT's First and Second Studios, the Gunst Drama Studio, the Chaliapin Drama Studio, the Armenian Studio, the Moscow Proletkult, and the Tchaikoʋsky Motion Picture Studio. Taking on another assignment seemed impossible, especially after Vakhtangov's poor health started to rapidly deteriorate. But, if anything, it was the Habima's lack of commercialism, its robust amateurism and sincerity, even its childlike innocence—made more human still by its constant infighting over theatrical doctrines and techniques—that ultimately attracted Vakhtangov to them.

After directing the Habima in a series of short one-acts in 1918, Vakhtangov decided to take up the study of Hebrew. While convalescing from one of his many bouts of illness in a Moscow hospital, he shared a room with an aged rabbi.

There, beginning with the Hebrew names of animals, Vakhtangov hoped to increase his vocabulary. Yet he learned with difficulty. When the rabbi quizzed him on the Hebrew word for horse, Vakhtangov fell silent. The old Jew slowly turned to face his student. Amazed by Vakhtangov's limited capacity to memorize, the rabbi reminded him of the word, "Soos! Soos!" as he incredulously stroked his head with two outstretched hands. The lesson for Vakhtangov was a revelation: the essence of Hebrew—the secret of Jewish communication—is in the hands. Unlike the manual signals of the Italian, Frenchman, or Russian, which in this circumstance would emphasize the pictorial image of a horse, the rabbi's gesture articulated his frustration with Vakhtangov. Jewish gestures reveal the speaker's hidden feelings about his subjects, his words, even the persons that he is addressing, but are not mimed images. Mastery of Hebrew was no longer necessary. In fact, since few Moscow spectators could comprehend it, Vakhtangov now found his lack of fluency advantageous. He could focus on the communication of thoughts through his performers' hands. Suler's yogic theory of Prana rays that radiate from the palms functioned automatically and unconsciously in traditional Jewish gestures. The amateur Habima could be a laboratory for another First Studio experiment.

"The Dybbuk"

The Dybbuk, a mystical play of possession and exorcism by the Jewish folklorist and historian, S. An-Sky (a.k.a.

Solomon Rappoport) was chosen as Vakhtangov's directorial vehicle for the Habima. Originally written in Russian,
but soon translated into Hebrew and Yiddish, *The Dybbuk,*
which was based on an actual case of demon possession in
southwestern Russia, detailed the Hasidic folkways in an
isolated nineteenth-century village. The music for the production also came from An-Sky's ethnographic research. As
with his previous treatments of the Chekhov and Maeterlinck
texts, Vakhtangov unmasked the hideous features of both the
fraudulent religious characters and their gullible bourgeois
followers in An-Sky's script. For Vakhtangov, *The Dybbuk*
was not merely a kabalistic legend about the vicissitudes of
love, but a mystery play that revealed the timeless features of
class struggle: a Jewish bride who is forced to marry the idiot son of a rich merchant becomes possessed by the spirit of
her impoverished lover.

At first Vakhtangov had relatively little time to work with
the idealistic Habima players, who were sorely in need of
basic actor training. Many of them stood rigid on stage, unable to relax or move. The elementary exercises of Relaxation and Concentration proved time-consuming and the results too limited for Vakhtangov's liking. He quickly re-
sorted to Affective Memory. He asked, when were they
most relaxed in their lifetime? During their weekly Turkish
bath before the Sabbath evening meal, they replied. Then
sensorily relive that experience, Vakhtangov demanded.
Blocked muscles and tensed bodies suddenly eased. The
Habima performers learned to relax.

The fantasy world that their characters had to inhabit also proved difficult for the Habima actors. Their early improvisations lacked depth and conviction. Vakhtangov asked one group of actors, who were supposed to tell occult stories about "wonder-rabbis" at the beginning of the play, to use the tales as substitutes for their descriptions of food. Immediately the lines took on a new dynamic meaning for the constantly hungry Habima performers. Images of animals (frogs, hyenas, monkeys, birds, cats) and objects gave each actor a basic physicalization. The performer enacting the wealthy merchant, for instance, patted and displayed his protruding stomach as if it were a huge bag of gold coins. Each intricate gesture and movement was carefully constructed and justified. An actor playing a beggar, using the image of a bird, struck a pose with one hand open with his palm coming out from his chest (the bird's claws) and the other hand flapping at the bottom of his spine (the tail). When Vakhtangov asked the actor for a Justification of his physical stance as a beggar, the actor could only refer to the bird imagery. Vakhtangov showed him that a real beggar might keep one palm upright, in front of his body, for begging directly from oncomers and the other hand open just behind his back in order to collect from others who have passed by. In this way the character of the beggar becomes fused with the image of a cagey crow. These Justifications made the most grotesque characterizations and stylized movements both real and alive for the performers.

Mounted in January 1922 in a tiny hall, *The Dybbuk,* in some ways, resembled Vakhtangov's other eccentric productions. His Theory of Contrasts, however, took on a much greater internal significance here. According to Vakhtangov, personality is only a balance of conflicting impulses. A shy person, for example, is shy because he is terrified of openly releasing his social aggressions. So when these opposing traits burst into violence, the attacker's neighbors are suddenly confounded. The quiet, bookish man who suddenly becomes a savage murderer is a tabloid speciality; the criminal who repents and joins a monastery is another. Each actor in *The Dybbuk* revealed such contrasting character features, usually in movement. They were told that the rhythm of the character follows the rhythm of these changes: a pathetically shy listener in the synagogue unexpectedly erupts with emotion, flinging his hands out of his long sleeves to tell a story; then realizing the inappropriateness of his sweeping gestures, he retracts his hands into his robes and meekly returns to his hunched position. Only Leah, the heroine of *The Dybbuk,* was to be played simply—in the purest MAT style—in striking contrast to the grotesque mannerisms of the other actors.

Vakhtangov's *Dybbuk* was an enormous success with Moscow's experimental theatre audiences. Meyerhold, Eisenstein, Tairov, Sergei Radlov and others were electrified by its bold and layered sense of rhythm and character. Entering the Habima's auditorium was like being dropped into a faraway and supernatural world. It was impossible to believe that the Habima Players were once amateurs. The MAT crowd, including Stanislavsky, was much less curious. In fact, Stanislavsky never saw *The Dybbuk*. After

Vakhtangov's death in May 1922, he came to the Habima for a performance, but the electricity, for the first time since the Revolution, had been cut in the theatre. Stanislavsky returned again in the fall and the power failed a second time. It became a standing joke, long after the Habima emigrated to Berlin and Tel Aviv in the twenties, that their Moscow space could not bear the charge of two stars: Vakhtangov and Stanislavsky.

Carlo Gozzi's "Turandot"

Vakhtangov's last production, Carlo Gozzi's *Turandot,* staged in the Third Studio a month after *The Dybbuk's* premiere at the Habima, is considered his greatest. Approaching death in 1921, Vakhtangov was determined to fill this production with all of his acting innovations. Unlike the Habima Players, the actors from his own studio, although young, were highly professional. He could drill them for long hours in complicated and advanced techniques. To begin with, *Turandot* utilized multiple styles of acting and performance. While *The Dybbuk* had but one mood (or two, if the character of Leah is counted), *Turandot* had mixed moods. It alternated from open sincerity to ridiculous clowning and improvisation (both feigned and real); from serious Stanislavsky-like Affective Memory to social parody and high theatricality. A riot of contrasting moods and forms prevailed. No audience had quite seen a production like *Turandot.* Even Stanislavsky and the entire MAT left astounded. Vakhtangov had truly transcended the discoveries of the First Studio.

Vakhtangov compared the audience's experience of theatregoing to that of eating in a restaurant. The pleasure of dining out is more than just eating, it is a special event. The unique environment of a restaurant, its service, the presence of other customers, the different dishes, even the tableware are important to the customer. The accumulation of such details makes going out an experience. Spectators should feel the same way about theatre, Vakhtangov told his studio actors. No restaurant attempts to disguise the fact that its patrons are in a restaurant setting. It does not ask them to pretend that they are back in their own kitchens. Likewise the theatre should never hide from its audience the fact that they are in a theatre. And like the doormen, hat check girls, waiters, busboys, and chefs of a fine restaurant, the actors and theatre workers must also remember that their function is to present spectators with an unique experience. Vakhtangov's notion of the "festival spirit" had finally found its expression in *Turandot*. He declared that there should be no fixed somber moodiness in the theatre, a la the MAT, only the feelings of joy and celebration.

For Vakhtangov's actors, the *Turandot* rehearsals marked the high points in their artistic and personal lives. Dozens of autobiographies published after the war would testify to this. Instead of costly Venetian or Chinese costumes (the Italian play is set in a mythical Peking), the actors made their own hand props, costume accessories, and clothing out of the most childlike and simple materials. A tennis racket became a king's scepter; a torn towel, a beard. Surely, this would remind Vakhtangov's audience that they had not stepped into a real Mandarin court of ancient China.

As he had in *The Dybbuk,* Vakhtangov perfected each gesture and thought of his actors. The improvisations leading to proper characterizations and the justifications were more complicated, partly because of the nature of the production, but also because of his performers' professional acting experiences. Here is a typical example of Vakhtangov's directorial ingenuity. One actress had difficulty playing the evil character, Adelma. The actress felt the character went strongly against her own nature. Vakhtangov told her to make the following Adjustment: she was not Adelma at all, but a Commedia dell'arte performer playing Adelma. In addition, her new Commedia character indulges in a fantasy where she is the wife of the director of the Italian troupe and simultaneously the secret lover of the leading actor. She wears torn shoes that are too big for her and loves playing tragic parts. But whatever she plays, she always finds an opportunity to hold a dagger. Instead of fighting the scripted character of Adelma, Vakhtangov's actress now had a whole new attitude and understanding of the role. The key to her interpretation was not her view of Adelma but of the Commedia character. Somehow this made the part playable as well as truthful for her.

Turandot began with the actors greeting the audience near the cloakroom and in the aisles. Four Commedia characters appeared on the stage, bantering with the audience about the show and the events from that day's newspapers. Then just before the curtain, Vakhtangov's performers, in evening dress, personally welcomed the crowd. To assure the audience that nothing would be hidden from them, the actors, in full view of the house, started to don their costumes and apply makeup to their faces. Singing extras, or zannis, quickly assembled the visually stunning Constructivist platforms and three-dimensional flats for the first scene. From that moment, every imaginable acting style, from melodramatic realism to quick improvisations, appeared in rapid succession as Gozzi's fairy tale unfolded. During an emotional monologue about the death of his beloved parents, which must have touched Vakhtangov's war-ravaged audience, for instance, one of the *Turandot* actors began to cry. Another actor ran on the stage to collect the tears in a wooden bowl. He showed the bowl to the spectators in front of him, proclaiming that the tearful performer was using an Affective Memory and it produced real tears! This was clear evidence of the power of Stanislavsky's System, he shouted over the audience's laughter.

The final dress rehearsal of *Turandot* on February 27th, 1922 created a sensation among its invited audience. Stanislavsky immediately ran to Vakhtangov's apartment during the first intermission. Bedridden with cancer, Vakhtangov was asleep. Stanislavsky left instructions for Vakhtangov to be wrapped in his blanket as if it were a toga; he deserved the sleep of a Roman conqueror. *Turandot* proved to Stanislavsky that his System had much wider applications. Three months later, at the age of thirty-nine, Vakhtangov died, leaving behind a studio and a new technique.

VAKHTANGOV'S EXERCISES (1919-1922)

How much Vakhtangov radically altered or transformed the Stanislavsky System's basic teachings is debatable. Nothing that Stanislavsky or Sulerzhitsky taught was rejected by their pupil. But by the early twenties, Vakhtangov's acting theories and methods appeared heretical to Stanislavsky's most devoted followers. Vakhtangov, it seemed, with his emphasis on the actor's physicality and the grotesque qualities in his productions, often at the expense of the play's logic, had gone the way of Meyerhold. Only after Turandot's *success and Vakhtangov's death did Stanislavsky realize that many of Vakhtangov's reformulations were valuable additions to his System training.*

Vakhtangov divided the actor's course of study into four parts: 1) Preparatory Work, comprised of sessions in Relaxation, Concentration, Justification, Fantasy, the Circle of Attention, The Task, Affective Memory, and Tempo; 2) the Method of Work, which consisted of exercises and études in Communication and Public Solitude, two System features that trained the actor to deeply interact and to live truthfully on stage; 3) Analysis of Plays and Roles; and 4) Outer Characterization, which included exercises in Rhythm.

Sources for exercises: *Transcriptions of Vakhtangov's* "Eight Lectures" *given at the Vakhtangov Studio in 1919; Vakhtangov diary entries (1917-20) (selections published in many books); Boris Zakhava,* Evgeni Vakhtangov and His Studio *(Moscow, 1926); Joseph Rappoport's arti-*

cles in the magazine Tear i Dramaturguria *(Moscow, 1931-
35); Serafim Birman,* The Actor's Work *(Moscow and
Leningrad, 1939); Nikolai Gorcharkov,* Vakhtangov and His
School of Stage Art *(Moscow, 1957); Raikin Ben-Ari,*
Habima *(NY, 1957), and 1987 interviews with Habima ac-
tor, Benjamin Zemach.*

RELAXATION

*A relaxed performer is better able to follow the precise
instructions of his director and not become involved in
extraneous, nervous movement. Relaxation and Concentration are often inseparable. Complete attention or
absorption on an object, sound, smell, feeling, or
thought will automatically free the body of self-consciousness and tension.*

1. Examine an object carefully, put all your soul into
   understanding it. Now listen completely to an isolated
   sound in the room or outside. Separate all the noises
   into clear categories. Next, smell an odor. Forget everything around you, just smell. Then feel the air, sense
   the pressure of your feet against your shoes, your shoes
   against the floor, the floor against the earth.

2. Sit in a chair, using only the necessary effort it takes to
   sit upright. Your arms, legs, neck, shoulders, and head
   should be totally relaxed. Slowly begin to tense the

muscles in one hand, then the whole arm. Continue to tense each part of your body. Then go back and reverse the process, relaxing each part individually.

3. Practice the above freeing and tensing routines in movement. For example, stand up and walk freely, but with your neck taut and stretched out like a goose.

CONCENTRATION

An actor must have an object of attention every moment that he is on the stage. Concentration exercises develop the actor's ability to find that object quickly and then be carried away by it.

4. Practice putting all of your attention into hearing a sound, touching an object with your fingertips, tasting a drink or some food. Fully concentrate on each of these separate activities.

5. Remember in precise detail how you spent the day—the places you went, the people with whom you spoke. While you do this, ignore your classmates around you who are trying to distract you.

6. *Mirror Exercise:* Standing face to face with another actor, mirror his every move. Concentrate on the smallest detail of his movement.

7. *Director and Actor Exercise:* The first person, "the Director," executes some simple movements. The second person, "the Actor," must then copy the Director's movements and expressions. After that, "the Director" demonstrates the mistakes of "the Actor." The two people then reverse roles.

8. All the student-actors sit in a row. The first person says one word, which the second repeats and then adds another word. This continues to the end of the row, and then back to the first person who repeats all of the words said, adding to the word chain. The exercise continues until the concentration and the order of the word chain is broken.

JUSTIFICATION

The actor must strongly believe in the reality of everything onstage. He can do this through Justification. Every physical object and movement must be justified, or brought into the actor's private world. Creating a personal, mental reality or relationship for all the things with which he comes in contact will ground the actor in the play and character. Otherwise, the actor will spend his time onstage ignoring some aspects of the performance or feeling dead when he can find no attachment to an activity or object.

9. *Living in the Pause Exercise:* Freeze your body in any position. Now repeat the pose, using one of the following justifications: 1) you are posing for a photographer, 2) you are dancing and the record has suddenly stopped and must be replaced, 3) you are in a restaurant and you hear someone talking about you, and 4) you are preparing to go to sleep and you suddenly hear crashing sounds coming from another room, which you try to determine is the result of a clumsy cat or a burglar.

10. Start to perform an action. Stop suddenly at the sound of a hand clap by your teacher. Remain in your given position, relaxing so you can easily maintain your balance. Now justify this pose. For instance, if you are sitting on your right calf with your left arm stretched out, the Justification could be that you are taking off a tightfitting boot and holding on to a pillar for support. Repeat the same action and pose, now thinking of the Justification as you begin it.

11. Enact three different and disconnected movements. Justify each one separately. Then justify the series together. For instance: 1) raise your right arm, 2) put it to your forehead, 3) put your left hand in your pocket. These could be justified as: 1) hushing an audience, 2) trying to remember your speech, and 3) searching your pocket for your notes. Together, these constitute the gestures of a nervous lecturer.

12. Justify the following accidents if they happened in a real performance: 1) unexpectedly finding a cigarette butt on stool, 2) hearing your partner laugh in the wings, and 3) waiting for your partner who has missed a cue.

FANTASY

Fantasy results from the marriage of Imagination and Naiveté. To fantasize, an actor must not only imagine his creation but also strongly believe in it. Children naturally fantasize, but actors need to justify their beliefs.

13. Add concrete details to any of the Justification exercises (See above). Using the example of the lecturer (Exercise 11), fantasize who the crowd is, what kind of speech you are giving, what you are wearing, and so forth. Act out a complete story using those poses, justifications, and new details. Try to keep your story within plausible realms.

14. Place a cap on the table. Imagine that it is a rat. Justify this perception. Picture the physical aspects of the rat: its size, color, shape. You must see the actual cap, but regard the size, color, shape as those of a rat's.

15. Now pretend the cap is a cuddly puppy. Imagine the brim is the puppy's muzzle, the cap's top as its back,

and so forth. Your relationship to it and your ability to perceive the puppy's physical properties will then endow it with reality. Create an attitude toward it: love, disinterest, disgust, etc. Show your attitude toward the puppy through your handling of the cap.

16. Look at a stool. Create an attitude toward it as if it were: 1) a beehive, 2) a kennel, housing a vicious dog, and 3) a huge basket of food.

17. Look at a stick on the stage. Create an attitude towards a stick as if it were: 1) a gun, 2) a snake, and 3) a musical instrument.

18. Find a letter on the table and read it. First decide whether it contains good news or bad news. In either case, imagine all the details in it: 1) who wrote it, 2) for whom is it intended, 3) what does it say, 4) what is the background of its contents, 5) who are you, 6) from where have you just come, and so forth.

19. With a partner, enter the stage. Start with an attitude in your relationship: 1) you hate each other, 2) you love each other, 3) you are afraid of one another, and so forth. Now begin to fill in the details and justifications as you act.

CIRCLE OF ATTENTION

In many ways, the Circle of Attention is identical with the First Studio's Creative Circle. Vakhtangov attempted to blend the work in Relaxation, Concentration, and Naiveté into a series of simple, focused manual activities. Instead of merely miming the handling of imaginary objects, the actor was told to concentrate on creating the reality of the action within a limited area.

20. Without the use of actual objects, execute the following actions:
    a. embroider a christening robe
    b. wash linen
    c. clean and shine shoes
    d. model with clay
    e. arrange your hair
    f. untie a small box of candy
    g. make a fishing rod and catch fish with it
    h. put out a fire
    i. get dressed
    j. clean a rifle
    k. glue a box together
    l. play with dolls

AFFECTIVE MEMORY

To recreate feelings and emotions, the actor must first practice developing his sensory awareness and abilities to recall physical sensations. Before an actor can use an Emotional Memory, he must master re-experiencing the simplest sensation and physical activity.

Exercises in Sense Memory

21. Lift a piece of cloth from the floor, using only the minimum amount of energy. First calculate, spontaneously and accurately, the exact amount of energy required to pick it up. Repeat this exercise until it is done perfectly.

22. Pick up a chair with the greatest lightness and freedom. Without a sound, lift it into the air, swing it around, and return it effortlessly back to its place. Repeat until performed flawlessly.

23. Reproduce the imaginary action of lighting a lamp without any visible objects. Remember vividly how a match is struck. Feel even the texture and weight of the match. Remember clearly how to remove the top of the lamp, the weight of its base and so forth.

24. Using only imaginary objects, perform the following actions based on your memory of doing them: 1) sewing a button on a shirt, 2) chopping wood, 3) heating a kettle of water, and 4) catching fish.

THE TASK

The Task resembles Stanislavsky's later ideas of Given Circumstances, Objectives, and Actions. Vakhtangov wanted to combine the actor's separate analytical, psychological, and physical instructions into a single playable unit. The Task of the actor consisted of: 1) finding the character's intellectual Goal, 2) feeling the character's physical Desire, and 3) making a stage Adjustment to the demands of the text and director.

25. Bang your fist on the table with the following justifications: 1) in order to quiet a meeting, 2) in order to test the firmness of the table, and 3) in order to frighten a friend who has fallen asleep at the table. Do not preplan the action of your activity—that is, how you will do it. In each action, concentrate on *why* you are banging the table.

26. Practice the following Tasks: 1) bringing a friend a present, 2) delivering bad news, and 3) scolding him. Work on developing the nature and occasion of the gift

(i.e., his birthday); who has sent the bad news, what the nature of it is; or why are you angry with him.

27. Using the given obstacles, perform the following scenes: 1) You meet your partner in your shared room. The two of you have quarreled and are not on speaking terms. Feeling that you are in the wrong, you decide to make up. 2) You start to clean up your room in preparation for studying, but your upstairs neighbors begin making a terrible racket that will prevent you from concentrating. 3) You dress and clean up your room because you are expecting company. Then you receive unpleasant news and have to leave immediately. 4) You come home with a newspaper which lists the winning results of a lottery. Your number is listed among the winners and you check a notebook to confirm the number. Now you cannot find the actual lottery ticket. You search everywhere in the room. Eventually you find it and go out to collect your winnings.

TEMPO

Like the First Studio's notion of internal Rhythm, Tempo expresses itself in physical activity with the increase or drop of energy. The major difference between Rhythm and Tempo is that the latter derives from the outside environment. In every scene and situation, the actor must find the appropriate Tempo.

28. Enact the following scene: you are eating in a railroad cafe. Establish a Tempo for it. Suddenly, a loudspeaker announces that your train will depart in five minutes. Observe the change in your Tempo as you eat.

29. Enact the following scene: someone is forcing you to scramble eggs. Notice your Tempo and energy level. Now scramble eggs to feed someone who is straving. Observe the natural increase in Tempo and energy.

COMMUNICATION

Vakhtangov closely followed Sulerzhitsky's ideas on the significance of nonverbal Communication between actors. Only through a concentrated Communication with his partners could an actor make a deep contact with his audience.

Études in Communication.

30. You are seated at the bed of a sick person. Silently you wait for the doctor. Watching the sleeping patient, you see his pain and sickness. Internally, you feel his suffering and want to help him. All of this must be apparent in your eyes.

31. In a room with your mother, father, and eldest brother, you are studying. At the window, unnoticed by them,

your friend's head appears. Silently and secretly, you try to signal him that you cannot meet him for a walk.

32. In a hospital room, your ailing father lies behind a curtain. Your brother, sister, and you silently wait for the doctor to come. Meanwhile, you bring water and medicine to your father. The three children are united by their love for their father, their sense of sorrow, and a common feeling for the physician.

33. Using the simplest words, you and your partner argue over a textbook. You have come to borrow it and he refuses to lend it. After reproaching one another and arguing over old accounts, you attempt to convince him to give you the book.

34. You are a watchmaker and your partner is a dissatisfied customer. He demands that you repair his watch again, without charge, while you maintain that he broke the watch himself. Use a minimum of dialogue.

35. At a river landing, you attempt to have the boatman row you across the river. Because a storm is coming, he refuses. An argument ensues. Again try to convince him with a few and simple words.

PUBLIC SOLITUDE

The actor's ability to act privately in public is a test of his skills in Relaxation, Concentration, and Naiveté. In this sense, Public Solitude takes the simple work of the Circle of Attention and brings it into a total theatrical environment. It is the actor's first exercise in "living onstage."

36. Using furniture or stage objects as substitutes (i.e., a chair as a shrub), create the real space for one of these environments:
    a. the forest
    b. the field
    c. a boat on the river
    d. your home

37. Now imagine you are alone in that environment. Add the smallest details which will enable you to perform your natural activities there. At first, spend only ten minutes in your environment. Then increase the time spent there by five minutes each time you perform the exercise.

RHYTHM

Although Vakhtangov's stage direction was noted for its fine sense of Rhythm and musical movement, his exercises in Rhythm followed a similar pattern to that of the First Studio.

38. Throw a piece of cloth in the air. Study how it falls and find its natural rhythmic movements. Practice throwing the cloth so as to add rhythmically to the richness of the fabric, color, and its "individuality."

39. Take hold of a piece of drapery. Begin to handle it in such a way that it appears to have a life of its own. Let the drapery vibrate so it seems that no human hand is touching it. In fact, it seems to be escaping from you.

40. As someone plays the piano, follow the changing musical rhythms, while performing one of these actions: moving the furniture, cleaning the room, cleaning your clothes, setting the table.

41. Find the national rhythm in movement and language of each of the following types: Frenchman, Englishman, Italian, Jew, and German.

CHAPTER FOUR

MICHAEL CHEKHOV'S REBELLION: THE RUSSIAN YEARS

Find out where he is performing and seek him out! Michael Chekhov is my most brilliant pupil.

Stanislavsky to Stella Adler, 1934

The nephew of the playwright Anton Chekhov, the actor Michael Chekhov spent much of his career developing a radically new technique built on Stanislavsky's principles. Christened Mikhail Alexandrovich Chekhov in St. Petersburg, he was part of the "generation of the '90s," a term used to describe Soviet artists who were born during the 1890s and who came of age at the time of the Revolution. Yet unlike Meyerhold and the other Russian theatricalists who broke from the MAT traditions, Chekhov shared many of Stanislavsky's concerns for the actor's emotional depth and spontaneity. But Chekhov felt both the master's teachings and those of Vakhtangov were primarily the creations of

117

directors and not performers. Therefore they ignored something that was precious to Chekhov: the super-imaginative and intuitive sides of acting.

APPRENTICESHIP AT THE MAT AND THE FIRST STUDIO

Joining the MAT in 1912, the twenty-one-year-old Chekhov was already an established character actor with the prestigious Maly theatre. Stanislavsky took a personal interest in the nephew of Anton Chekhov, often inviting him to dinners, which Chekhov vividly remembered as a series of directions on how to add character and emotional qualities to the act of eating a meal. On one occasion, for instance, Stanislavsky coached him on how a man might eat soup after hearing about the sudden death of his child. Within a few months, Chekhov was invited into the MAT's First Studio. There, Chekhov fell under the direct tutelage of Vakhtangov. Their personal and professional relationship, although close, was filled with complications and rivalries that often manifested in practical jokes, some of which led to real violence. On tour in the spring of 1915, for example, the two roommates created a game, "The Trained Ape," whereby they took turns each morning acting the part of the "ape." The "ape" crawled out of bed, while remaining on all fours, and prepared the coffee. Until the breakfast was fixed, the other had the right to beat the "ape." For Chekhov, and maybe for Vakhtangov, too, the game had deeper psychological implications. Finally, the ape-Chekhov "mutinied," and an actual fight broke out, with Chekhov losing a tooth and Vakhtangov almost suffering from asphyxiation.

During the MAT's 1912-13 seasons, Chekhov appeared as walk-ons in various productions, including the Gordon Craig *Hamlet*. During one performance of Molière's *The Imaginary Invalid*, Stanislavsky reprimanded young Chekhov for "having too much fun with the part" as one of the supernumerary physicians. Chekhov was shocked by the master's admonishment. Wasn't *The Imaginary Invalid* a comedy? Therefore, wasn't a certain element of fun called for? While professing perfect belief in Stanislavsky's System of acting, Chekhov found himself in trouble with its creator from the very start.

Cast by Richard Boleslavsky in the First Studio's test production, *The Wreck of the "Good Hope,"* in 1913, Chekhov created quite a stir. He took the minor role of Kobe, the idiot fisherman, and transformed him into a creature of pathos and intense lyricism, altering the character, through movement and makeup, from a low comic type into a sincere and morbid seeker of the truth. For the audience, Chekhov's minor role became a new focus in the play. But when criticized that his notion of Kobe was not what Herman Heyermans, the Dutch playwright, intended, Chekhov replied that he went beyond the playwright and the play to find Kobe's true character.

The idea that an actor can "go beyond the playwright or the play" is the first key to understanding the Chekhov Technique and how it differed from Stanislavsky's early teachings. Chekhov claimed that the impulse "to go beyond" came to him during his earlier apprenticeship at the Maly Theatre. During a 1910 performance of Nikolai Gogol's *Inspector General,* Chekhov watched one of his teachers, Boris Glagolin, in the lead part of Khlestakov. Suddenly, a revelation, a "kind of mental shift," overtook Chekhov: "It became clear to me that Glagolin plays the part of Khlestakov not like others, although I had never seen anyone else in that part. And this feeling, 'not like others,' arose in me."

Over a period of time, Chekhov's acting goals changed. The "conquest of the audience" at the Maly and the relaxed and "truthful" portraits of the MAT gave way to a quest for extraordinary character interpretations. In a sense, Chekhov had turned Stanislavsky's acting training on its head. Instead of the System's two-part Work on Oneself followed by Work on One's Role, Chekhov made Imagination and Character Work his primary foundation. In the Chekhov Technique, every other kind of exercise would follow from them.

One apocryphal story may explain the theatrical and personal conflict between Stanislavsky and Chekhov. Asked by the teacher to enact a true dramatic situation as an exercise in Affective Memory, Chekhov recreated his wistful presence at his father's funeral. Overwhelmed by its fine detail and sense of truth, Stanislavsky embraced Michael, thinking that this was yet another proof of the power of real Affective Memory for the actor. Unfortunately, Stanislavsky later discovered that Chekhov's ailing father was, in fact, still alive. Chekhov's performance was based not on recapturing the experience, but on a feverish anticipation of the event.

Reprimanded once again, Chekhov was dropped from the class due "to an overheated imagination."

With every First Studio production, Chekhov's imaginative creations found a growing number of fans. For Vakhtangov's *The Peace Festival* (1913), Chekhov prepared the role of Fribe, the family drunk, in his usual novel manner. Working against the standard portrayal of an alcoholic, Chekhov built the physical character on a madman's realization that each part of his body is dying in a separate and horrifying way. Chekhov believed that death on the stage should be shown as a slowing down and disappearance of time in the human psyche. He wanted the audience to feel this physical retardation and even see the point where the slowing tempo ceases altogether as the character vainly fights off death. It was a coup de theatre.

The First Studio's adaptation of Charles Dickens' *Cricket on the Hearth* in 1915 established both the artistic legitimacy of Sulerzhitsky's troupe and Chekhov the performer. Cast as Caleb, the frightened, but kindly toymaker, Chekhov insisted on personally inventing and building all the mechanical toys for the production. His character came to him slowly as he visualized an old man seated on a chair and began to imagine the character's every action. Blending Dostoyevskian morbidity with an all-embracing Tolstoyan love for his blind daughter, Chekhov's Caleb proved equal to Vakhtangov's villainous and mechanical Tarelton. Nowhere else was the constrast between the two actors more clearly evident than here. Stanislavsky singled out Chekhov's performance as "almost brilliant."

At the end of 1915, Vakhtangov directed a First Studio production of Berger's *The Deluge*. Double-casting himself and Chekhov in the part of Frazer, the bankrupt American merchant, their rivalry continued. Much to Vakhtangov's displeasure, Chekhov saw Frazer as a confused, but loving Jewish businessman although the character's ethnic background was nowhere indicated in the play. Using his hands to slap at the air like an hysterical girl and stumbling bent-knee against the saloon furniture, Chekhov was criticized for his overly physical and grotesque interpretation. Admittedly, Chekhov developed his character around an unusual mental image: Frazer was a man who unconsciously wanted to break through the clothes and skin of his competitors in order to make the deepest human contact possible; he wanted to physically touch their hearts. Yet, between the interpretations of Chekhov and Vakhtangov, the audiences clearly preferred Chekhov's creation. In fact, Vakhtangov soon began to imitate Chekhov's Frazer as did other First Studio actors who later played the part. After two productions, Chekhov's Russian fans grew to several thousand.

SPIRITUAL CRISIS

Between 1913 and 1923, Chekhov appeared in twelve MAT and independent productions, usually as a lead or in important supporting roles. His reputation as an actor and independent thinker increased dramatically during this period. But bouts of depression brought on by alcoholism, family deaths, war fever, revolution, and civil war often undermined his mental equilibrium and ability to act. Yet the first two years after the Bolshevik victory (1918 and 1919) were especially crucial to Chekhov's spiritual and artistic breakthroughs.

During the run of the First Studio's *Twelfth Night,* Chekhov was reduced to a "gaunt brooding soul, weighed down by Russia's sorrows," according to Oliver Sayler, a visiting American critic. Played in his characteristic style of sharply etched contrasts, Chekhov's Malvolio was very much a crowd pleaser. In Chekhov's opening night performance, Shakespeare's sweet lyrical sensibilities became enmeshed in Malvolio's "swamp" of horrifying eroticism. But within a few weeks of the *Twelfth Night* premiere, Chekhov developed acute paranoia, believing that he both could "hear" and "see" distant conversations across Russia. Fears of suicide and his mother's death prevaded his daily activities. By the spring of 1918, Chekhov's immediate family situation had deteriorated. His wife Olga divorced him, taking away their newborn daughter. Stanislavsky had a team of psychiatrists examine his overwrought, but still favorite, actor. Finally, Chekhov underwent a series of hypnotic treatments, which eased the worst of his episodes of depression. Chekhov discovered, however, that he was subject to fits of uncontrollable laughter, which sometimes erupted in the middle of his stage performances.

More than the advanced psychological therapies of Stanislavsky's physicians, it was his encounter with Hindu philosophy and Rudolf Steiner's Anthroposophy that altered Chekhov's psychic condition. In fact, Chekhov's passionate investigation of Steiner's "spiritual science" filled a dangerous void in Chekhov's creative world. It unblocked his choking emotional life. Gradually, Chekhov understood that his maddening lack of will was the residue of a spiritual crisis rather than the physical fatigue of an overworked actor. Chekhov began to reason that his poorly timed breakdown —at the height of his fame—was actually his soul's silent protest against what he was becoming as a performer: "a malevolent vessel of drunken egotism." In many ways, Chekhov in 1918 resembled the Stanislavsky of 1906. Both were praised as performers, but were intensely unhappy as individuals and artists. Each longed for a more perfect system of actor training. Only Chekhov sought a more perfect style of communion with the audience. Chekhov dreamed of a new acting mode that contained a larger and deeper component, more akin to the ecstatic religiosity of the ancient Greeks than the petty commercialism and politics in the theatre of contemporary Russia.

During the war years, disciples of Rudolf Steiner, called Anthroposophists, performed private demonstrations of Eurhythmy, or the "science of visible speech," in Moscow. These spiritual dances, which attempted to transform sound and color into movement, made a tremendous impression on Chekhov. Like the mantras and various yogas of South Asia, Steiner's sound and movement exercises provided his religious followers with a sophisticated and clearly delineated artistic outlet. Outside of Russia, at Anthroposophical centers in Germany and Switzerland, performances that utilized Eurhythmy—either as pure dance or as acting movement in Steiner's own Mystery Dramas—attracted a wide following. Although Chekhov did not meet with Steiner until 1922 during a Central European tour, his contacts with local Russian Anthroposophical groups were frequent and productive. More important, they stimulated Chekhov's ideas for a visionary theatre. Marrying the inner truth and emotional depth of Stanislavsky's System with the beauty and spiritual impact of Steiner's work became Chekhov's obsessive quest.

THE FIRST CHEKHOV STUDIO AND THE CHEKHOV TECHNIQUE

In 1918, Chekhov opened his own studio in the Arbat theatre district of Moscow. It was the first of several such attempts to pass on his singular form of acting. Of the hundreds of students who auditioned every autumn between 1918 and 1922, thirty were chosen each term. Normally only three remained by December. Chekhov rarely prepared a class. The Studio work emphasized his experiments in character development. In his private flat, Chekhov investigated the concept of reincarnation and the techniques of Indian yoga. One novel exercise involved deep meditation. Tapping their minds' collective or racial unconscious, the students tried to reincarnate themselves as their characters. If a performer playing Hamlet, for instance, could somehow mentally metamorphose himself into the actual Hamlet, Chekhov felt a whole new chapter of actor training and spiritualism could be written. Few students, to be sure, shared Chekhov's personal beliefs and enthusiasm for the occult.

Yet in his Studio, Chekhov also invented a vocabulary that spoke more directly to the performer's thought process and imagination. Stanislavsky and Vakhtangov normally told actors what they wanted from them in abstract terminology, i.e., "to concentrate," "to act naively," "to feel heat." This caused the performer to reinterpret each command according to the workings of his mind and body. The instruction "to relax," for instance, a frequent directorial request, often produced a number of secondary responses in the actor's mind before physical relaxation could be achieved. For example, an actor may think the following: "Although I feel relaxed, the director has said that I am not. Therefore, some part of my body must be tense. First I must determine where. I'll start with my shoulders ..." Chekhov's Technique dealt primarily with images, especially visceral ones, that short circuited complicated and secondary mental processes. So, instead of telling the actor "to relax," Chekhov asked him "to walk (or to sit or stand) with a Feeling of Ease." The notion of the "Feeling of Ease" offered an outward, positive image for the actor and replaced Stanislavsky's directorial command, "to relax." Another example: rather than demand that a slouching performer, playing a proud aristocrat, "sit up straight," Chekhov told him to let his body "think up.'" While the differences between Chekhov's linguistic approach and that of his teachers may seem slight to the non-actor, for Chekhov they were crucial cues, showing a profound understanding of how the actor thinks and responds.

Both Chekhov and Stanislavsky believed that actors must

be given ways to go beyond the acting clichés and theatrical banalities that they inherited from older generations of established performers. For Stanislavsky, this meant that the actor had to look for "truth" in real human behavior or in the logic of human psychology. For Chekhov, the secret lay somewhere outside the theatre and life, somewhere deep in the performer's imagination. According to Chekhov's teachings, it is the stage's ineffable, magical elements that truly bring the actor and spectator together: the field of energy, or liveliness, that radiates from the actor's creative work; his profound and startling character choices; the kinesthetic sensation of perfectly executed corporal movements and sounds all create a special and powerful atmosphere—the pure atmosphere of the stage. The MAT's tired naturalism could be found everywhere in the streets, in daily life itself, so the theatre had no need to compete with that. Instead, Chekhov's challenge to Stanislavsky prophesied a new kind of performance style that used acting as a charged or mystical form of human communication.

More than anything else, Chekhov's work became associated with the power of the imagination. Since the theatre's strength lies in its ability to communicate through sensory imagery, rather than through literary ideas, Chekhov sought to uncover appropriate actor training devices that would heighten his students' imaginative awareness. His improvisations, which constitute the bulk of his early teachings, advanced the notion that scenic space could have a special, almost bewitching, aura filled with evanescent or intoxicating Atmospheres. Stanislavsky and Vakhtangov's Emotional Recall exercises were based on the actor's sensory memory of an actual event from his life. Chekhov schooled his students to find fictional, external stimuli from outside their personal experiences that could fire their emotions and imaginations.

During the start of Lenin's NEP period of limited capitalism (1921-27), the Chekhov Studio suffered financially. The productions of fairy tales and literary adaptations that Chekhov and his students offered interested only a limited audience. To survive, therefore, Chekhov was forced to return to acting on the professional stage. Before the demise of his Studio in 1921, however, Chekhov played a trick on Stanislavsky. Since starting his System, Stanislavsky cautioned all his students and fellow teachers never to reveal any details about their work. Although Stanislavsky had many critics outside the MAT, none could point clearly to any single feature of his training because so little was known about it. Only hearsay, rather than specifics, could be reported and criticized. But in 1919 Chekhov published a detailed analysis of Stanislavsky's work in two issues of the workers' cultural journal, *Gorn*. Stanislavsky and the First Studio members were outraged. For two reasons: one, because Chekhov broke Stanislavsky's firm prohibition, and two, because Chekhov mischievously attributed some of his own extreme ideas to the master.

UNDER VAKHTANGOV'S AND STANISLAVSKY'S DIRECTION

Two years later, however, both Stanislavsky and Vakhtangov forgave Chekhov. Early in 1921, Chekhov starred in Vakhtangov's gloomy, expressionist *Erik XIV* by August Strindberg. Playing a young and socially impotent king of a corrupt Swedish court, Chekhov discovered the character's internal nature in rehearsal by continuously thinking of one startling image: Erik is trapped inside a circle. His arms dart out of the circle, attempting to touch something. But Erik finds nothing. His hands are left hopelessly dangling and empty. Inspired by the lessons of Eurhythmy, Chekhov "found" his role by playing with the shape and quality of the character's movement and by rearranging his physical stature and shape. Only when he "saw" the character's gesture did Chekhov begin his embodiment, or Incorporation, of the role. Using a purely external image, rather than an Affective Memory, Chekhov created the character of Erik in a non-Stanislavskian and striking manner.

Simultaneous with *Erik XIV,* Chekhov was rehearsing the lead role in Gogol's *The Inspector General* for the MAT, under Stanislavsky's direction. The master director dominated his young performers, often stopping them midway through a sentence and then demonstrating his own personal acting choices. But Chekhov's private interpretation of Khlestakov was so unusual and his physical characterization so bold—"a malicious pixy from another world"—that even his First Studio companions were amazed. Stanislavsky did not try to improve upon Chekhov's choices.

On opening night of *The Inspector General,* a shocked Vakhtangov whispered to Stanislavsky, "Can this be the same man we see in our Studio every morning?" Vakhtangov, who had been working with Chekhov on the *Erik XIV* project, now hardly recognized him in the Gogol character. Some spectators remarked that Chekhov brought a nuanced and strange lightness to the part. The sick, pathological, and flippant traits of Khlestakov perfectly and frightfully knitted themselves into a fresh interpretation. There is no doubt that Stanislavsky and others appreciated Chekhov's finished productions. What concerned the MAT crowd was Chekhov's erratic means of creating a character. Every night his performance had a totally different feeling to it. His stage actions were improvised on the spot. But more than that, Chekhov's character had a tendency to shift and refocus from performance to performance. It was as if Gogol's Khlestakov, once given life on stage, began to direct the actor Chekhov.

THE SECOND MAT

In 1923, after Vakhtangov's untimely death and the MAT's celebrated tour of Western Europe and America, Stanislavsky rewarded Chekhov with the directorship of his own theatre, the Second Moscow Art Theatre. Freed of financial worries, Chekhov began to experiment in earnest. Exercises in rhythmic movement and telepathic communication filled the actors' crowded training and rehearsal schedules. In preparation for a controversial *Hamlet,* Chekhov taught his actors to use Shakespeare's language like a physical property, tossing balls as they rehearsed their lines. Chekhov announced to his cast, "If the System of K.S.

[Stanislavsky] is high school, then my exercises are university." Neither the actor's own personality nor stage clichés of a director or playwright were allowed to become the basis of any role. Chekhov claimed his Hamlet, sometimes independent of his commands, varied from one performance to another in response to the unconscious needs of his audience. Some saw the Second MAT's experimental production as a symbol of the Russian intellectual's political dilemma in the midst of the contemporary workers' state.

In the presentations that followed *Hamlet,* Chekhov demonstrated his legendary ability to transform himself from one physical type into another. For the Second MAT's production of *St. Petersburg* (1925), with its apocalyptic atmosphere based on Andrei Bely's Symbolist novel, Chekhov played the old Senator Abeleukov who refuses to believe that the Czar's old order is about to collapse. Chekhov spoke of finding his Archetype, or "correct" image, for the character in the movements and sounds of "loneliness." Although he seemed more a leading actor than an artistic director at the Second MAT, Chekhov's approach soon became the subject of severe government criticism. In Alexander Sukhovo-Kobylin's *The Case* (1927), he began to incorporate aspects of animals and supernatural beings into the physical embodiment of his character, Muromsky. In his preparation, Chekhov attempted to make "contact" with a vision of Muromsky, asking him questions and imitating his responses.

By 1927 Chekhov was officially denounced as an "idealist" and mystic because of his use of Eurhythmy and

his interest in Steinerism, now completely forbidden in Soviet culture. Protesting Chekhov's techniques, seventeen
performers left the Second MAT. Immediately following the
split, the foremost Moscow newspapers branded Chekhov
"a sick artist" and his productions "alien and reactionary."
Within the year, he was marked for liquidation. But Chekhov's popularity and luck held. His work in film and the
publication of his autobiography created support for him
even within the government and GPU, the internal secret
police. In August 1928, after receiving an invitation from
the Austrian director Max Reinhardt to perform in Germany,
Chekhov was given permission to emigrate with his family.
He immediately left for Berlin. It was there that Chekhov
began a second phase of his career, his "wandering years," a
period of mixed professional and personal successes.

MICHAEL CHEKHOV'S RUSSIAN EXERCISES
(1919-1928)

Before the mid-thirties, Chekhov had no formalized technique or acting regimen. He did, however, create many sets of exercises and improvisations. Some had a lightness and even a festive feel to them, particularly the Imagination exercises. For the most part this was intentional. In order to open up new areas of the actors' minds, Chekhov made training fun. The internal censors that prevented many actors from attempting new ideas and roles, so as not to appear stupid or ridiculous, stopped once the work was framed in a childlike, risk free way.

Chekhov also developed units of exercises called Threshold, or Creative Spirit, that produced a rush of exhilaration and energy in his students. For Chekhov, the loss of mental energy and enthusiasm was one of the greatest obstacles to the creation of character and a sense of liveliness on stage. A few aspects of his training followed the System's pattern, for instance, the sessions in Concentration and the Feeling of Ease (replacing Stanislavsky's Relaxation). But even these were taught along more physical and imaginative lines by Chekhov. Other features of the Chekhov Technique fell into more distinct and unique categories: Movement/Eurhythmy, the Feeling of the Whole, Atmospheres, Characterization and Working with the Text.

Sources for these exercises: Michael Chekhov's MAT 2 rehearsal notes of Hamlet *(1923); Chekhov's two autobiographies,* The Path of the Actor *(Moscow-Leningrad, 1928) and* Lives and Encounters *(1944-5), originally published in the New York Russian language magazine,* Novi Zhurnal; *Deirdre Hurst du Prey's transcriptions of Chekhov's first discussions at Dartington Hall, England (1935-37); and 1985 interviews with Seinya Silverman, a student of the Chekhov Studio in 1920 and 1921.*

THRESHOLD/CREATIVE SPIRIT

The Threshold is an imaginary boundary that marks the division between everyday life and the world of the Creative Spirit. It is symbolized by a line or circle. Once the actor crosses it, he steps into a magical environment where any thought or action is possible. His artistic and spiritual energies can become fully liberated.

1. *Actors' March:* March around the room following a leader. Think to yourself: "I am strong, I am healthy. My hands and arms are free and beautiful, my legs are strong." Imagine yourself divided into three parts: 1) around your head is the feeling of space and power, the power of thought; 2) around your chest, the power of feeling; and 3) around your feet, the power of will. Keep marching in a circle until these three are in perfect harmony.

2. Continue the *Actors' March*. Say to yourself: "I am light. My arms are like wings," lifting your arms at the same time. Then say: "I can fly." At this point, begin to run with the thought: "My body is light, my arms are wings, I can fly."

3. Sit down as if "you are creating something." Get up in the same way. You may, for instance, imagine that you have just solved an age-old medical problem that will change society, or that you have just completed a great painting.

4. Try the same movement ten or twenty times until you know the feeling of creation. Move with your entire being so that there is energy through your body and around it.

5. Take one sentence and repeat it twenty times as a work of art. Say the same thing with just your hands and then in fuller gestures. You can speak this sentence out loud. Now "touch" it, and then try to "think" of it as a solid form. To give it the feeling of art, not chaos, you must open your soul and allow the Creative Spirit to manifest itself through your words, movements, thoughts, and feelings.

6. Try to realize a purpose for every thought and action in your life. Once this is accomplished, let the Creative Spirit increase your everyday awareness.

CONCENTRATION

7. Listen to the beat of a drum. Feel it around you, enveloping you. You will feel joy from concentrating on this sound. When the actual sound stops, continue to "listen" to it. Follow the sound in your head until it is as clear as the drumbeat itself.

8. Look at the whole room or everything on a table. Shut your eyes, remember each object in detail, and then describe them. Repeat this lesson every day until you have perfectly described every object.

9. Concentrate on a spot in the room. "Send" yourself to it, become one with it. When the spot becomes a living force in your imagination, move about the room, play ball, becoming freer in your body, but all the time increase your focus toward the spot. Now drop your concentration on the spot completely. Yet remember how you felt when you were perfectly concentrated.

10. Pick up a small object—an eraser, for instance. Concentrate on it for fifteen minutes, taking in its shape, its color, what it does and does not do. As you put the object down, experience a feeling of power over it. Your head should feel wonderfully clear. Then think of the image of the object attached to some part of your body, the base of your spine, for example. Then shake it off and move it to another part of your body.

IMAGINATION

In Chekhov's Moscow Studio, Concentration and Imagination exercises resembled one another. With the Concentration exercises, however, the actor's process of focusing on and remembering the object was important. In the Imagination exercises, Chekhov emphasized the detailed recreation of the object itself.

11. Look at some object in the room and then close your eyes. Try to keep it very clearly in your mind's eye. Mentally recreate this object as precisely as you can. The energy you will spend on this work will develop your imagination.

12. Imagine a flower growing from the seed in the ground into a full plant. Closing your eyes, follow the process of its growth and development.

13. Imagine a horse going backwards or a person drinking a glass of water in reverse.

14. Imagine a tree and a house. Try to transform the tree into the house without breaking the images or adding new elements. Or imagine a chair turning into a cow. Meditate on them, gradually merging the images.

15. Listen to some music and create an image at once. This image can be a remembered object or not. Keep it im-

movable. If no image comes immediately, invent one.

16. Take an abstract idea, like truth, and from that create a living image in your mind.

FEELING OF EASE

The Feeling of Ease is a substitution for Stanislavsky's Relaxation. Chekhov felt that actors could respond more easily to positive directives or imagery, rather than abstract commands. The words "Feeling of Ease" suggest airy and graceful images of the body in harmonious motion or stasis.

17. Remember the feeling of your body when it had almost no weight at all. Now just lift your arm and experience the desire to become lighter. Try to lose the weight of your body. Feel your arms as wings. Repeat lifting your arms, acheiving the weightless quality twice as fast. Then enact raising your arms only in your imagination. When you have no heavily weighted arms and hands at all, only arms and hands supported by invisible strings, your body will lose its weight entirely.

18. Practice moving with the Feeling of Ease. Carry a chair with the Feeling of Ease. Sit with the Feeling of Ease. Stand with the Feeling of Ease. Run softly with the Feeling of Ease. Collapse with the Feeling of Ease.

MOVEMENT

All stage Movement is psychophysical. The mind and body are locked together. The mind must "move" with the body. The actor should become newly aware of his body through special, almost naive, physical work. None of the following Movement exercises should resemble repetitive gymnastics or military drills.

19. *Staccato-Legato:* Thrust your upper torso and head in the following directions: right, left, up, down, forward, and back. Your arms and fingers should extend in the direction of the thrusts. At the start of each lunging movement, think that you are throwing your "soul" across the room. This will add energy and focus to the exercise. In the first cycle, each motion is performed to sharp staccato (lightning) rhythms. Then it is repeated with flowing legato (watery) rhythms. The movements cannot be mechanical. The actor's mind and body must follow the same rhythmic motion.

20. Play an imaginary game of ball. While you are tossing the ball, become aware of the different parts of your body that are being used.

21. Human movements are almost always the result of some external or internal command. For the first time in your life, move without thinking. Make meaningless movements.

22. Convey the word "flower" without words. Speak with your hands, arms, with your whole body. Now communicate the action, "pick up the stone." The gestures you make should transform themselves into speech. Find very simple gestures that, afterwards, work their way into your speech. In broadly defined gestures, try to find the whole thought. Without illustrating, try to give every word a gesture.

23. Become familiar with the sense of scenic space. Begin to distinguish between your right and left sides; then, your front and back. Be conscious of the straight and curved lines your body creates when you move. With your hands and body, draw lines and figures in the air and on the stage floor. Make large, expressive, and beautiful gestures with your whole body.

Eurhythmy

A form of dance-movement invented by Rudolf Steiner in Germany before World War I, Eurhythmy has spiritual, aesthetic, and therapeutic values and functions. Through the abstract movements of the human body, Eurhythmy communicates unspoken words, colors, sounds, moods, rhythms, and ideas. A highly coded system with a specific vocabulary of gestures, Eurhythmy is an attempt to express the "eternal soul" of the performer through images and motion. Like the nineteenth-century French philosopher Francois Delsarte before him, Steiner trisected movement into Will,

Thought, and Feeling.

24. *Eurhythmy of Vowels:* Integrate the following sounds, movements, feelings, and images:

Vowel Sound	Movements	Feelings/Images
Ahh	arms raised over head in "v"	awe/man's discovery of the sun
Aaa	arms crossed over chest (as in "ray")	contraction/protection of family
Eee	right arm raised in salute	power/energy streaming to sky
O	arms out in a ring	sympathy/embracing the world
Uuu	parallel arms straight out	anxiety/piercing mystery of the world

25. *Steiner's Trinity:* 1) lift your heel from the ground by the power of your Will; 2) lift your foot from the floor and step forward, as if you are Thinking; 3) place your foot down with Feeling.

26. Lift your foot with a quality of "power." Then with the thought of the "future." Finally with a feeling of "doubt."

27. Touch things in a creative way. You must have a real feeling for form and truth in each motion.

FEELING OF THE WHOLE

An artistic work must have a finished form: a beginning, middle, and end. Equally, everything on the stage must convey this sense of completion and totality. The Feeling of the Whole is strongly felt by an audience and must become second nature to the performer's work.

28. Find the "spine" in everything you do on the stage. For instance, when you play tragedy remember that your whole body is "filled with tears." If it is a comedy, you must be "laughing inside" so that the audience will be laughing with you.

29. Say a sentence or create a short movement as if it were a complete piece, with a pause at the beginning and at the end (e.g., "The trees are in flower."). Deliver the words or gestures as if they were actual objects. Wait for your audience to "catch" them.

30. *Living Statues:* Your group is given a theme (e.g., Love, War, Russia). Entering one by one, each of you freeze in a dynamic position, creating a living piece of sculpture. Noting carefully the artistic composition as he enters, each student must find his place in the Feeling of the Whole.

ATMOSPHERES

An Atmosphere is an invisible or transparent medium, like fog, water, panic, fear, or darkness. A single Atmosphere can envelope the entire stage space. Its heightened mood unconsciously affects both the performer and spectator as its unseen waves are felt and absorbed by the actor and then radiated to the audience. The play or its director suggests the Atmosphere of a scene, and the performers work together to create and maintain it. In Chekhov's Studio, Atmospheres took the place of Affective Memory and Emotional Recall.

31. Enter a room. Be conscious of the air in the room. Breathe it, absorb it. Now let the air become "light." After a few minutes, let the air turn into a specific Atmosphere, like "happiness." First breathe in "happiness." Experience it, feel it. Later breathe in the Atmospheres of "sadness," "fear", "humor," and so forth.

32. Enter a room, where an imaginary burning fireplace creates the Atmosphere. Breathe in the fumes. Let your imagination now create the room's reality.

33. With a group, play that you have just entered the scene of a street accident. Someone has been run over by a

car. Without knowing exactly what has happened, take in the Atmosphere of the scene. Breathe in the "air" of confusion and calamity.

34. Enter an imaginary old church. Walk through it, taking in its Atmosphere. Let your body naturally react to your internal imagery.

CHARACTERIZATION

35. Lie on the floor with your eyes closed. Breathe deeply. Slowly realize that you have been transformed into your character (e.g., Hamlet). Somehow, like magic, you have been reincarnated as your character. Try to figure out how it happened. When you are ready, and only then, stand up as your character.

36. Create an image of your character in your mind. You might begin with a single part of his body (e.g., long side whiskers) and then assemble the total physical image, part by part, until it is complete. Now attempt to "imitate" your image. Then, remaining separate from him, speak to your character, observe him, find out about him.

WORKING WITH THE TEXT

37. While someone reads the text of a play, throw a real ball—in character—to the intended "receiver" of each of your sentences.

38. Transform the sound of each word in a text into movement. Forget the meaning of the word. Instead, find the right spiritual colors buried in the music of the word.

39. Convey the meaning of the words in a text with movement and a ball. Be conscious of the new sensations in your body as the text and motions blend.

40. Under the guidance of the director, rehearse the entire play in your imagination. Run through every scene for yourself and your partners in your mind.

CHAPTER FIVE

MICHAEL CHEKHOV IN EXILE

Chekhov's training was deep and exacting. He made us feel the importance of theatre. Gave us pride in being actors. Taught us our responsibility to the audience. It was the most happy and creative time of my life. A time that gave me the foundation that sustained me in a long career.

Beatrice Straight, 1982

Arriving in Berlin in the late summer of 1928, Michael Chekhov started a second phase of his career, a voluntary exile across Central, Western, and Eastern Europe. For seven years, most of them filled with disappointments, Chekhov pursued his lifelong quest to create his own troupe and method of actor training outside of Soviet Russia. But in every adopted country where his acting was highly praised, Chekhov's grandiose plans for a theatre studio or school stalled, backfired, or disintegrated. The traditional curse that plagued other Russian artists-in-exile—that no nation outside Mother Russia would fully embrace and un-

147

derstand them—doggedly pursued Chekhov wherever he went.

WITH MAX REINHARDT

His first professional encounter abroad, with Max Reinhardt in Berlin, left Chekhov depressed and confused. Hoping to play a solo Hamlet on the German stage, Chekhov was cast instead as Skid, the broken-hearted husband of a rising Broadway starlet, in Gloryl Watters' and Arthur Hopkins' jazz-age play *Broadway,* retitled *Artists* in Europe. Already successful in Berlin, Reinhardt arranged for a second production with Chekhov to be staged in Vienna. Now set in a circus-like arena in one of Vienna's largest theatres, *Artists* opened in February 1929. Everything about the production upset Chekhov: the short and sloppy rehearsal process, the general lack of direction, and, most of all, his own uninspired characterization. During *Artists'* shaky premiere, however, a strange vision came to Chekhov: he saw the character Skid beckoning him to sit in a certain way, to speak in a new pitch, to move more slowly, to look with greater power at his wife. Chekhov interpreted this revelation in a personal and mystical way: "Fatigue and calm turned me into a spectator of my own performance.... My consciousness divided—I was in the audience, near myself, and in each of my partners." His acting in *Artists* was enthusiastically received, ensuring Chekhov a new career in the German-speaking world. Within one year, he appeared in three major German films.

ACTOR AND DIRECTOR IN BERLIN

Chekhov called his visionary sighting of Skid, Divided Consciousness, since it resulted in a dual awareness of simultaneously following his character's guidance while performing before an audience. In his last Soviet production, *The Case,* he had tried to conjure up the image of Muromsky. But only in Vienna did the character manifest itself naturally and fully. The phenomenon of Divided Consciousness that Chekhov felt, however, may have been more related to the sensation of performing in one language while thinking in another than it was to any intense spiritual state. Obeying the Higher Ego, or stepping outside oneself to comply with the character's demands, became Chekhov's new credo. When Chekhov later explained this concept to Stanislavsky that spring in a Berlin cafe, the master became startled and perplexed. Furthermore, Chekhov admonished Stanislavsky for creating a harmful system of actor training, contending that Stanislavsky's heavy reliance on Emotional Recall devices led actors into uncontrolled hysteria. Suddenly their former pupil/teacher roles were reversed. Chekhov recommended that Stanislavsky replace Affective Memory with pure Imagination. Of the mind's three active phases (dreaming, thinking/remembering, and imagining), Chekhov lectured Stanislavsky, only imagination was truly effective in the creation of art. To the heat of Chekhov's passionate insistences, Stanislavsky could only disagree.

In 1930, Meyerhold and other Soviet theatre artists visited Chekhov in Berlin, with the intention of persuading him to return to Moscow. Back in the Soviet Union, Meyerhold even joked to his actors about a plan to kidnap Chekhov. During this time, Chekhov himself was busy with Eurhythmy and Anthroposophy, attending Rudolf Steiner centers in Germany. But also stranded in Berlin, in self-imposed exile from Russia and Palestine, were the Habima Players. They approached Chekhov, a fellow émigré from Russia and the MAT, and begged him to direct them in a Shakespeare play. Chekhov selected *Twelfth Night* yet soon realized the youthful and overly serious disciples of Vakhtangov were anything but naturally comic performers. For them, Chekhov invented a series of Lightness exercises, which they attacked with their typically zealous fervor. By the time the play opened, the Hebrew *Twelfth Night* had a light, airy texture. Newspapers from around the world favorably reviewed the Habima's foray into Shakespeare. And Chekhov's reputation as an innovative director became known in France and the English-speaking world.

THE WORK IN PARIS

By early 1931, Chekhov began to think of leaving Berlin. He started work on a "compact" and modern dress *Hamlet,* in which Claudius and Gertrude ingeniously played themselves and the Player King and Queen. Then several other projects were offered to Chekhov, like the directorship of two newly formed Russian-language theatres in Prague and Paris, but each of them collapsed financially. But Paris alone contained the largest Russian-speaking population outside the Soviet Union. In the spring of 1931, Chekhov made Paris his new home.

Both pro- and anti-Bolshevik factions of the Russian émigré world in Paris joined forces to oppose Chekhov's theatre plans. Russian and French supporters of the Soviet Union viewed the nephew of Anton Chekhov as one more renegade bourgeois actor, seeking material riches in the West; his repertoire eschewed contemporary politics, favoring nineteenth-century comedies and occult dramas. In addition, slighted that Chekhov refused to speak out against Communism or sign their petitions, the powerful Russian anti-Bolshevik factions accused Chekhov of being an agent of the GPU (the Soviet secret police). The few short evenings of Russian-language plays and sketches that Chekhov did mount in Paris, however, found support in the politically moderate French press. Still, technical imbroglios and budgetary mismanagement complicated each production.

THE CHEKHOV-BONER THEATRE STUDIO

With the financial assistance and producing skills of Georgette Boner, a young pupil of Max Reinhardt, Chekhov eventually established his own theatre studio in Paris. At the end of 1931, it opened with a mystical pantomime, created by and starring Chekhov. It was based on Alexei Tolstoy's fairy tale, *The Castle Awakens*. Concentrating on Symbolist-like decor and musical effects as well as Eurhythmic movement, Chekhov hoped the production would attract a large international audience. Dozens of special exercises and études were created to train his young actors. Wanting to avoid the problem of performing exclusively before the Russian émigré community or playing in badly accented French, Chekhov invented a "universal language" for *The Castle Awakens,* using the ideas of Rudolf Steiner. In fact, the sparse text consisted of only fifty lines of fragmented German.

Promoted as a mystery parable of modern life, *The Castle Awakens,* if anything, revealed Chekhov's hidden fantasies in 1931 and their symbolic transformation. One psychological interpretation that could explain Chekhov's ferocious attachment to the folk drama follows: In the ancient Castle (Russia), a faithless Servant (Bolshevikism/materialism) lulls both the King and his Courtiers (the Russian people) asleep with his song. Outside the Castle, Prince Ivan (Chekhov) discovers Beauty (Anthroposophy/Second MAT), which he delivers to his father, the King. Immediately, the evil Bone Spirit and his Daughter (Soviet government/cultural commissars) come to steal Beauty away. The frightened King wants to give up Beauty, but Ivan hides her. The puny Ivan is then defeated in a lopsided battle with the Bone Spirit and his Daughter, and the Servant leads the evil forces to Beauty, who kidnap her. Prince Ivan decides to leave the safety of the Castle in order to retrieve her.

In the Forest of Poets (Europe), Ivan fights with the Forest Spirit (Reinhardt/Boner), but then saves his life when the Forest Spirit becomes entangled in a Witches' web (European commercialism). Later the Witches deprive Ivan of his powers to hear, see, and speak, but the Forest Spirit returns to rescue his senseless friend. Using his special contacts with the elements, the Forest Spirit revives all of Ivan's faculties, especially his power of speech, which now has a greater force (German language). Together, the Forest Spirit and Ivan seek out the captured Beauty, who is weighted down with stones in the Bone Spirit's fortress. The two heroes defeat the Bone Spirit and his singing Daughter and go back to the Castle. Once again, the Servant steals Beauty away, but, through trickery, Ivan kills the Servant. The Castle awakens to the wedding of Ivan and Beauty.

Although acclaimed by much of the Parisian and foreign press, opening night difficulties with the set and stagehands and the play's occult theme damaged *The Castle Awakens'* reception with the theatre-going public. Once more, Chekhov's dream was failing. Highly sensitive to criticism, Chekhov never again experimented with the creation of texts for his "future theatre." And after this experience, Anthroposophy became a largely private concern in his life and work.

Boner and Viktor Gromov, one of Chekhov's Russian assistants, managed to secure positions for him at the state theatres in the independent republics of Latvia and Lithuania in 1932 and 1933. A handful of former First Studio and MAT 2 members found their way to the Baltics and joined Chekhov's troupe. Now back in Eastern Europe, Chekhov briefly enjoyed stardom as both an actor and master teacher. Performing in Russian, while the other actors played in their native languages, Chekhov finally overcame his linguistic

barriers onstage that plagued his early wandering years. But
the threat of war and a fascist coup, in addition to a growing
xenophobia in the Baltic republics, sent Chekhov and his
Russian colleagues temporarily back to Western Europe and
then, at the invitation of the impresario Sol Hurok, to
America.

CHEKHOV ON BROADWAY

Renamed the "Moscow Art Players" by Hurok, Chekhov's group opened a season on Broadway in the Spring of
1935. Over the diplomatic protests of the Soviet embassy in
Washington, Hurok hoped that the Russian actors would be
mistakened for the original MAT. The deceptive title and
advertising campaign proved to be unnecessary. Chekhov's
eccentric characterizations and fine direction of Russian and
Soviet classics took the American theatre intelligentsia by
storm. A faction of the Group Theatre, led by Stella Adler,
considered asking Chekhov to fill their newly vacated directorship. (Lee Strasberg and Cheryl Crawford had just
resigned.) Adler, who had worked with Stanislavsky the
previous year in Paris, remembered the master's dictate to
seek out Chekhov wherever he might be performing. And
now the stateless Chekhov had fallen into her hands. In
response to the the Group's pleading, Chekhov presented a
lecture-demonstration on his Technique in September 1935.
While Oliver Sayler, a noted authority on the Russian theatre, translated, Chekhov outlined the basic features of his
teachings, especially as they related to Characterization. The

session is significant because it gives the first clearly stated examples of Chekhov's work since his exile from Moscow.

CHEKHOV ON THE CREATION OF CHARACTER

Chekhov declared that the end product of all actor training is the development of the stage character. He observed that the Stanislavsky actor has been taught to build his role on the similarities between his personal history and that of the character in the play. But this constant repetition of the actor's own nature in creating different parts over the years causes a progressive "degeneration of talent." The creative means are used less and less. Eventually, the actor will begin to imitate himself, relying, for the most part, on repeated personal mannerisms and stage clichés. Like Stanislavsky and Vakhtangov, Chekhov had touched on a fundamental problem of acting: the limited range of the standard actor's characterizations. Yet Chekhov's solutions, as outlined in the 1935 lecture, were considerably different from theirs.

Archetypes

To begin with, Chekhov said, the actor must define the specific type of character he is to play: "Tough Guy," "Angry Woman," "Sexy Girl," and so forth. These models, or Archetypes, are found in human nature. The playwright develops the individual variation within the type. But it is the function of the actor to make the character-creation come alive. The very first step an actor should take is to find the difference between himself and his character. What is the character's mind like? Does he think faster or slower than me? Is his understanding of the world clearer or more vague than mine? Are his emotions fuller than mine? Is he more passionate? Is his will more persistent and unyielding than mine? Once these questions are answered, a deeper and more specific understanding of the actor's character will result. In addition, observations of real people are useful. Watching and defining their unique differences can help the actor develop his character's features.

Centers

Chekhov maintained that every human body has an invisible Center. One can envision an imaginary cord anchored to a person's Center that pulls him forward. It guides or directs his movements through space. The Center is also an area, inside or outside the body, that physically reveals individual personality traits. If we watch people on the street and study how they move, we can locate their Centers and get a glimpse of their personality. Finding someone's Center, therefore, helps us intuit his hidden psychology.

Centers can be found in the chest, forehead, bridge of the nose, left shoulder, or any other part of the body. Centers can also have qualities: they can be large or small, dark or shining, warm or cold, wet or dry, aggressive or tranquil, colored or clear. Centers can also be static or moving, shape-changing, or appear in several places at once.

Since all people have Centers, Chekhov explained, then every stage character must have one as well. For instance, a selfish or proud character can have a Center located under his chin. The Center could be easily shifted to the upper lip, lower spine, or a left eyebrow. These changes transform his body shape and movement. The placement of a Center in different body parts establishes different kinds of selfish or proud characteristics. A selfish character with a Center in his upper lip speaks and reacts in a different manner than the same character with a Center in his lower spine.

An actor can physically create an inquisitive and nosey character, for example, by thrusting the back of his neck forward and then by variously placing the inquisitive character's Center: 1) at the tip of his nose, 2) in his eyes, or 3) by one ear. He will have then created three different kinds of nosey characters; an old nosey woman, for instance, could have a cold, hard needle-shaped Center on her left cheek. Other examples: a humble character may have a hollow Center in his chest; a cowardly individual could have a Center hanging just below his buttocks; a good and kindly character might place his Center in other people's hearts; and an aggressive man could watch his Center jumping out and clinging to other character's faces.

Imaginary Body

Every character has a physical body separate and different from that of the actor portraying him. Therefore the actor must sketch, in his imagination, the physical features of his role. Are the character's arms longer than the performer's? Is his neck shorter? And so forth for each part of the body. This helps create an Imaginary Body, the physical result of how the character-actor should look on stage. Of course, if the actor is very tall and the Imaginary Body of the character very short, then the completed stage persona will have be a new creation midway between the physical and the imaginary. But by communicating with the character, playing with him, asking him questions, the actor may discover the means to incorporate his Image. For instance, short persons normally look up to taller people, so finding a way to always look upwards at a partner will create the physical and psychological illusion of being short, regardless of the performer's natural height.

Personal Atmosphere

Finally, the actor must add Personal Atmosphere. Like Atmospheres of space (i.e., a Gothic church), Personal Atmospheres radiate moods and feelings. They are the immediate qualities that one receives from individual characters, like rigidity, lightness, efficiency, and so forth. For instance in *Twelfth Night,* Malvolio imparts the Atmosphere of pretention; Sir Andrew Aguecheek is filled with an Atmosphere of foolishness. When creating these, Chekhov stated, it is important for the actor to use the imagination in a free, even humorous way.

Like Stanislavsky and the MAT in Moscow, the Group Theatre was uncertain of how to react to Chekhov's explanation of his technique. There were no doubts about Chekhov's extraordinary acting skills, but another question arose: Could his technique be taught to others? Stella Adler and Bobby Lewis were excited about many of Chekhov's concepts. They would later utilize some of them in their own teachings. But most of the Group thought that Chekhov's theories were too extreme. Some left-wing members jokingly suggested that he be sent back to Russia.

MICHAEL CHEKHOV THEATRE STUDIO AT DARTINGTON HALL

Backstage after the Moscow Art Players' Broadway premiere, another young actress tried to get Chekhov's attention. This was Beatrice Straight. In her, Chekhov at long last found a sensitive and talented benefactor. With her friend, Deirdre Hurst (soon to be Chekhov's secretary), Straight invited Chekhov to Dartington Hall, the site of her family's estate and a progressive educational institution in Devonshire, England. In 1936, amidst other experimental projects in agriculture, music, small craft industry, and modern dance, Chekhov set the foundation of his new theatre. There, in Dartington's utopian community (created nine years earlier by Straight's stepfather and mother,

Leonard and Dorothy Elmhirst), the trio of Chekhov, Straight, and Hurst recruited instructors and students to study the Chekhov Technique. Drawn from the United States, England, Canada, Australia, New Zealand, Germany, Austria, Norway, and Lithuania, two dozen young actors were to become the initiates of Chekhov's twenty-five-year-old dream.

Except for the concept of Psychological Gesture, Chekhov's essential format had been articulated by 1937-8, Dartington's second term: Imagination and Concentration, the Higher Ego, Atmospheres and Qualities, "The Four Brothers," Centers, the Imaginary Body, Radiation, Significance, Contact (Ensemble Work), and Style. Later adjustments and changes were made at his American studios. The training there was thorough and deliberate, lasting two full years.

In England, Chekhov turned much of the technical apparatus of the Stanislavsky System upside down. As always, he was mostly concerned with the special physical nature of the actor's movement and the creation of new and startling characters. Chekhov shared with Stanislavsky a belief in developing the actor's sources for inspiration, feeling, and expressiveness, but he taught that the stimulus should always begin outside the private and internalized world of the performer. At Dartington, simple exercises in "The Four Brothers," the Feeling of Ease, the Feeling of Form, the Feeling of Beauty, and the Feeling of the Whole schooled the performer in special psychophysical movements, forcing him to think about his body in theatrical space like a choreographer or dancer would.

Chekhov's most radical innovation at Dartington was the further development of his substitutions for Stanislavsky's Sense Memory and Emotional Recall. Sensory stimulation came from the creation of Atmospheres and Qualities, or external expressions, which, when added to movement, provoked the feelings they mimed. To create anger in a character, for instance, a student would be instructed only to "add the Quality of anger" to his gesture or movement rather than search for a past or internal motivation.

The marriage of Imagination, Atmospheres, and Qualities supplanted Stanislavsky's Affective Memory for Chekhov's students. For example, to awaken, or to capture, the sensation of sadness, actors were told to do the following: 1) to imagine the grieving sounds of a rural family mourning the accidental and gruesome death of a boy and a girl; 2) to walk through the Atmosphere of a flood-devastated village; or 3) to sit and stand with a "Quality of sadness." Here, without having to consciously evoke difficult to control memories of personal experiences, Chekhov felt his performers could produce more powerful and individualized emotional expressions.

The Dartington period (1936-39) was a creative and happy time for the faculty and students, punctuated with high and intense artistic aspirations. Famous theatre and dance personalities, like Paul Robeson and Uday Shankar, visited the classes, but the creation of a professional theatre ensemble in England never materialized. There were other problems. Despite his mastery of English after only six months, Chekhov refused to perform on the British stage. Then England's anticipation of war with Germany in 1939 caused the Chekhov Theatre Studio to cease operation and relocate across the Atlantic in Ridgefield, Connecticut, a rural community not far from New York City.

CHEKHOV THEATRE STUDIO IN AMERICA

The bucolic conditions at the Ridgefield Studio in 1939 resembled those at Dartington Hall, yet its proximity to the New York theatre changed Chekhov's way of thinking about his school and means of instruction. First of all, the Studio felt its reputation would be enhanced with a successful New York production. So Chekhov allowed himself to be lured by George Shdanoff, a friend and director, to mount a large scale Broadway production of an adaptation of Dostoyevsky's *The Possessed*. They decided that studio actors, including newly recruited American ones, but not Chekhov himself, would perform in it. Yet *The Possessed* neither demonstrated the Chekhov Theatre Studio's particular skills in acting nor its public relations abilities. It was compared, unfavorably, with the ensemble work of the Theatre Guild and Group Theatre. Few reviewers saw the effort as that of a new young American group's first theatrical endeavor. And had the hastily staged *The Possessed* succeeded, the Chekhov Technique might have found immediate and widespread support in the New York theatre community.

Shakened, but not crushed, by the commercial failure of *The Possessed,* the Chekhov Theatre Studio continued to undertake productions. Between 1940 and 1942, the Studio mounted three highly acclaimed and hugely ambitious seasons of classical plays and comedies. Performing in repertoire, the young actors toured outside New York City, to New England, the Midwest, and the Deep South. Not since the days of traditional barnstorming theatrical tours in the teens and early twenties had most of the towns on their itinerary seen live and serious dramatic entertainment. The unusually high quality of the acting was noted in very nearly every county and city newspaper. A young and vibrant Yul Brynner played the lead in the Studio's *King Lear.* Yet that first Broadway fiasco haunted Chekhov. So he thought about bringing the Studio to New York in order to teach special classes for professional actors.

In the fall of 1941, the Chekhov Theatre Studio moved from Connecticut and opened on 56th Street in New York. The transfer to Manhattan brought Chekhov to a critical point in his long and unpredictable career. Was he primarily a teacher, actor, or director? It had been over a decade since Moscow and Berlin theatre critics had heaped praise on him as a performer. Yet Chekhov was determined to change the style of American acting. Only at his Studio could Broadway actors be retrained in his new Technique. Only there, Chekhov believed, could he directly influence the American theatre.

In addition to classes in the Chekhov Technique (conducted by Chekhov, George Shdanoff, Alan Harkess,

Beatrice Straight, and Deirdre Hurst), a full curriculum of speech training, Eurhythmy, music appreciation, choral singing, fencing, gymnastics, and makeup was offered at the Chekhov Theatre Studio in Manhattan. The twice-weekly, two-hour classes for professional actors, however, occupied a special place in Chekhov's thinking. Here he hoped to perfect and summarize all the elements of his Technique, in particular those related to Psychological Gesture, his last and most widely discussed acting invention.

THE PSYCHOLOGICAL GESTURE

Chekhov believed that Psychological Gesture was the key into the actor's subconscious. A concentrated and repeatable movement or action, the Psychological Gesture awakens the actor's inner life, and its kinesthetic image feeds him while he acts on stage. Every character, according to Chekhov, possesses a single Psychological Gesture, which reveals his secret, innermost motivation and personality trait. Before doing anything else, the actor must unravel his character's Psychological Gesture. Weeks or months may pass before the correct Psychological Gesture comes to the performer.

The movement that forms the basis of the Psychological Gesture may be as abstract and fantastic as an arm stretching endlessly through an imaginary prison window (Michael Chekhov's Psychological Gesture for Hamlet); or as concrete and realistic as the stroking of a cat while softly speaking of the heartless destruction of Russia's gentry (a gesture traditionally associated with Lenin). The Psychological

Gesture frequently guides the actor in his rehearsal choices and stage action. It can also function as a purely internal image, hidden from the director or spectator. It is "the actor's secret." Through the Psychological Gesture, Chekhov wrote, the soul of the character and the physical body of the performer meet.

CHEKHOV IN HOLLYWOOD

In 1942, the Chekhov Theatre Studio in New York disbanded due to the wartime draft and financial problems. Determined to promote his Technique further, Chekhov wrote the manuscript for a textbook, *On the Actor's Technique*. But the publishers, Harper Brothers, rejected it as too impractical and mystically oriented. In the same year, Chekhov left New York for Hollywood. (Eleven years later, Harper published *To the Actor* in a greatly reduced and revised version that is still in print today.)

Between 1943 and 1954, Chekhov played character parts in nine Hollywood films. Basically, he was seen as a comic or eccentric East-European type. In the film *Cross My Heart,* typically, Chekhov was cast as a mad Russian actor. Chekhov's character, in the role of Hamlet, having already killed one Claudius performer on stage, attempts to murder others unfortunate enough to be playing the King. In 1945, after receiving an Academy Award nomination for his role as the psychoanalyst in Alfred Hitchcock's *Spellbound,* Chekhov resumed teaching his Technique to young

Hollywood actors. Marilyn Monroe, Jack Palance, Anthony Quinn, and Akim Tamiroff were among his small cadre of students. In 1955, Chekhov, at age 64, died of heart failure in his Hollywood home. (Beatrice Straight founded a second Michael Chekhov Studio in New York City in 1980, which continues to teach the Chekhov Technique.)

THE CHEKHOV TECHNIQUE EXERCISES
(1937-1952)

Between 1937 and 1942 at Dartington Hall, England, Ridgefield, Connecticut, and New York City, Michael Chekhov devoted considerable amounts of energy and time to devising a full curriculum for training in his Technique. Instruction at the Michael Chekhov Theatre Studio lasted two years, with many classes in improvisational and scene work as well as thrice weekly sessions in movement, voice, and speech, including Rudolf Steiner's Eurhythmy. Classes in the core aspects of the Chekhov Technique were held every day. The exercises below comprise one year's study in the Technique.

Sources for these exercises: Stella Adler's notes of Chekhov's New School lecture (1935); Deirdre Hurst du Prey's transcriptions of Chekhov's classes given at Dartington Hall (1936-38; du Prey's transcriptions from the Chekhov Theatre Studio classes given in Ridgefield and New York City (1939-41); Chekhov's Russian-language textbook, On the Actor's Technique *(NY, 1946); and interviews from 1982 to 1987 with the following instructors and students of Chekhov's Paris, Dartington, and Ridgefield schools: Georgette Boner, Blair Cutting, Deirdre Hurst du Prey, Eleanor Faison, Felicity Mason, and Beatrice Straight.*

IMAGINATION

1. Look closely at a painting, a piece of sculpture, or a photograph of an architectural structure. Take in all of its special features of composition, sense of color, weight, and function. Enjoy its sense of beauty. Now imagine some elements changing: the colors or shapes transformed (the columns of a building, for instance, becoming three times as tall). Playfully think about these new artistic images by changing them. The results may seem ridiculous, but should always retain a sense of truth.

2. After reading a Shakespeare play, let your imagination rewrite or rearrange its plot, language, and characterizations. Do the same thing with a fairy tale.

3. Try to create something that does not exist: an animal, a flower, a landscape, a figure. It should be something of your own creation which you have never seen. Keep the image very simple. Create this in your imagination: You are walking through a forest. It is becoming dark and gloomy. Suddenly a very small, strange being appears before you. Create this being.

4. In very concrete detail, imagine a child. Then, remembering the facial details, imagine this person again as an old man or woman.

5. In one minute's time, imagine the same person again as young and then transform him into someone older. Don't start your transformation with a fixed image in mind. Give your imagination a free reign.

6. Imagine you are pouring tea into a cup, then imagine the action only in reverse.

7. Think of an episode in a fairy tale, like a castle transforming itself magically or a prince turning into a spider. Every day add more events with fresh and surprising details.

CONCENTRATION

8. Choose a chair and find out everything about it; its form, weight, color, etc. Say to yourself: "I see the chair," "I see the color," and "I am concentrating on the chair." Be one with the chair.

9. Send your feelings to the chair. Move it with invisible hands, touching it, and lifting it. Send your will, your power to the chair. Drop your concentration for a moment and become aware of the difference between concentration and non-concentration. Repeat sending your feelings and will to the chair. Increase the powers of Concentration.

10. Concentrate on the chair. When you feel you are one with the chair, close your eyes and see it in your imagination. Send your will, feeling, power to the image.

HIGHER EGO

The individual performer is always limited by his past experiences and habitual way of doing things. But the actor can learn to break out of his private, repetitive patterns and choices. Appealing to the Higher Ego, the source of artistic energy, allows the actor to temporarily leave his personality behind and expand his range of theatrical ideas and physical activity. From the Higher Ego comes the inspiration to create new and surprising characters.

11. Choose a simple action, like cleaning a room, searching for an object, setting a table. Repeat this action as least 20 or 30 times. Each time create a new way of performing the task. Avoid repetition in any way.

12. Study a character from a play that you know well. Then try to imagine the role performed by different actors you admire. Look for their inner and external approaches to the character interpretation. From their choices, you can learn the special qualities of each

actor. This will also teach you about your own special creative qualities in acting.

13. Discover what types of positive or negative impulses are present in every play. For instance, what kinds of evil do King Claudius, Cornwall, Edmund, Iago, Polonius, or Richard III symbolize? In what way might their opposing and positive characteristics be expressed? Where are the positive qualities of Claudius, Caliban, Rosencrantz? How can Edmund, Iago, and Queen Gertrude be played with charm?

14. Imagine your director is watching you. Incorporate his imaginary suggestions. Allow his imaginary presence to assist and clarify your work in rehearsal.

ATMOSPHERES AND QUALITIES

Atmospheres are sensory mediums, like fog or fear, that radiate from environments and people. Although they cannot be seen, Atmospheres can be felt strongly and are a primary means of theatrical communication. The Atmospheres of a Gothic cathedral, a modern hospital, or a pauper's cemetery influence anyone who enters those places. They become enveloped in the Atmosphere. People also give off Atmospheres of tension, hate, love, foolishness, and so forth.

Qualities refer to simple feelings or ideas that an actor can express physically: anger, joy, frustration, frenzy.

15. Imagine the air around you being filled with a certain Atmosphere, like fear, joy, tenderness, or horror. After a period of time, without forcing yourself, realize that the Atmosphere has entered your body, like a perfume or smoke that you have inhaled. Move and speak inside the Atmosphere. Now radiate the Atmosphere outward. Let its power increase as you once again absorb it.

16. Perform an action, like crossing the room. Now repeat the movement with different Qualities: 1) in a staccato or legato rhythm; 2) with calm, anger, or thoughtfulness; 3) fiercely, hastily, or slyly; 4) with a hard or soft feeling. Repeat your movement with each Quality until a feeling enters inside you.

17. Studying different objects or living things, ask yourself what gestures do these inspire in you. Combine the gesture with a Quality. For instance, a cypress tree may inspire an upward movement; add to that a pensive quality. A tiger lily may inspire a wide thrusting motion; to that, add a quality of violence.

18. Repeat the movements and Qualities until you experience an emotional reaction from them. Now, while remaining still, imagine performing the actions with the

Qualities. Continue to do this until you can naturally produce a complete feeling without actually moving.

THE PSYCHOLOGICAL GESTURE

The Psychological Gesture is a physical movement that awakens the actor's inner life. It serves as a key to the essential or hidden features of his character. Psychological Gestures may be large or diminutive in size, abstract or natural, but they are always simply executed. A character may only have one Psychological Gesture. In performance, the actor need only think of the Psychological Gesture to feed his internal characterization. Whether or not he physically presents the Psychological Gesture on stage has little importance.

19. Choose a play, even one that you don't know well. Imagine a performance of it, concentrating on the most expressive moments. Pick a character and talk with him in your imagination. Ask him to act before you and discover his goals and desires. Watch how the character is performing. From his action only, intuit his Psychological Gesture and then physically perform it yourself.

20. Alternate between performing the character's action and executing his secret Psychological Gesture. Add various Qualities to the Psychological Gesture if help-

ful. Retain the feeling and image of the Psychological ·
Gesture in your heart.

21. Take a sentence and speak it as you enact a Psychological Gesture. Now guess what Quality naturally belongs to the Psychological Gesture.

22. Slightly change the Psychological Gesture (i.e., letting your head tilt a bit or bending one knee), and notice how it suggests a new Quality. Through this exercise you should begin to discover the relationship between your outer movements and inner feelings.

23. Take a normal pose, like resting your head on a table. Then see what psychological meaning and Qualities are hidden behind this position. Concentrate on these secret feelings. When ready, improvise from your pose.

24. Use a musical piece to inspire an appropriate Psychological Gesture. Create another Psychological Gesture from another song. Enact both movements, harmoniously connecting them, and from that create a third Psychological Gesture without music. Going back to the first Psychological Gesture, once again improvise new ones until you have a connected string of them. Now let the Psychological Gestures resemble normal acting movements. This will add a new depth to your acting.

"THE FOUR BROTHERS"

"The Four Brothers" refers to four linked psychophysical movement skills: 1) the Feeling of Ease, which is akin to Stanislavsky's Relaxation work; 2) the Feeling of Form, which trains the actor to become an outside creator of his body movement, like a choreographer or sculptor; 3) the Feeling of Beauty, which brings the actor into the sphere of pure motion and being, like a dancer; and 4) the Feeling of the Whole, which helps the actor find the aesthetic totality over the development of scene or character, like a playwright or painter.

Feeling of Ease

25. Take the Feeling of Ease inside you. Walk up and down as you develop it. Don't allow your body to become rigid or stiff. Walk with your mind "outside your body" (observing yourself), and try to see which parts of your body are absolutely free.

26. *Flowing:* Walking in a circle, move through the space as if you were flowing in water. Each movement of the limbs should flow imperceptively into the next as if you were swimming. Each movement should be light and effortless.

27. *Flying:* Continue the above exercise but imagine yourself becoming lighter than air. As you spread your arms, suddenly you are levitating in the air. Then you are flying.

The Feeling of Form

28. Raise your arms and hands, experiencing a Feeling of Form. Lie down and then get up with the Feeling of Form. Be aware of your body weight; its lightness and heaviness. Increase the feeling of weight and add staccato and legato qualities. Add music.

29. *Molding:* Walking in a circle, make abstract shapes in the air with your hands, arms, and legs. Then with your whole body. Mold the air as if it were made of a heavier, clay-like substance. Now perform any activity, inwardly retaining the feeling that you are molding the air.

The Feeling of Beauty

30. Understand, as an absolutely new idea, that you have a body. Repeat the statement, "I have a body!" Raise your arms slowly, lower them, bend forward, to the side, backwards. Walk a few steps, raising your arms at the same time, remembering that your body is a thing of beauty. Kneel or lie down on the floor. You should feel that your body is receiving energy from the

earth and, therefore, is a medium for conveying artistic ideas.

The Feeling of the Whole

31. Say a sentence or create a short movement as if it were a complete piece, with a pause at the beginning and at the end. (e.g., "The trees are in flower.") Deliver the words or gestures as if they were actual objects. Wait for your audience to "catch" them.

32. Facing each other, two actors strike different poses. To the sound of music, they then move four steps forward, forming new complementary poses, which they hold for two beats and then continue moving again into a new position.

33. Without any forethought, start with the image of "Yes" (pronounced with wrath and power) and improvise a conclusion that will bring you to softly spoken "No." Repeat this, beginning with very short études, going from "Yes" to "No" and then allow the scenes to build in size with a substantial middle section.

34. With a partner, improvise a scene with one of you starting from the image "Yes" (going to "No") and the other beginning from "No" (going to "Yes").

The Four Brothers Together

35. Take a chair, carry it across the room, and sit in it. First do it with the Feeling of Ease, then repeat it with the Feeling of Form, next with the Feeling of Beauty, and finally with the Feeling of the Whole.

CENTERS

Every character has a Center. This is the imaginary area inside or outside his body that leads him forward. The Center may be any shape, size, color, or consistency. A single character may even have more than one Center. Finding a character's Center can lead to an understanding of his entire personality and physical being.

36. Imagine that there is a string fixed to the middle of your chest. Now begin to walk as if you are being pulled by that string. Execute other activities, like carrying a suitcase or moving furniture, but always remembering the pull of the string on your Center.

37. As you are walking in a circle, place your Center in other parts of your body: 1) the top of your head, 2) your left ankle, 3) your stomach, 4) below your buttocks. Notice how each Center changes your overall personality.

38. Continue to walk, but let the Center take on new shapes and sizes: 1) a hard red ball, 2) a flashing green light, 3) a soft beachball.

39. Now experiment with having several Centers. For instance, a normal circular one for the jaw and a pointed needle-like one in the left thigh.

IMAGINARY BODY

To create characters with different physical features from his own, the actor must first visualize an Imaginary Body. This Imaginary Body belongs to his character, but the actor can learn to inhabit it. Through constant practice, the performer can change the length and shape of his body and physically transform himself into the character.

40. Conjure up the physical body of another person, like a woman coming out of church. Think of your body stepping inside hers. Place a Center anywhere in this Imaginary Body and add Qualities. Move in the Body and create appropriate activities. Now add speech.

41. Imagine, then inhabit, the Imaginary Body of a character from a play.

42. Create five different characters and their Imaginary Bodies in thirty minutes. Add characteristic speech and activities.

OBJECTIVES

Like Stanislavsky and Vakhtangov, Chekhov believed that it was crucial for the actor to learn how to analyze and break down the actions of a scene. Chekhov's exercises in Objectives closely follow those of Stanislavsky.

43. Divide any scene into Objectives or aims for your character. Discover how the character will achieve his Objective by defining his Psychological Gesture.

44. Observe people on the street and attempt to discover their current aims, or Objectives.

45. Improvise a scene where your Objective is in conflict with your partner's. For example, you want to prevent him from sending a letter. Add different Atmospheres to the improvisation.

RADIATION

Seemingly a radical and typical Chekhov teaching, the work in Radiation at the Chekhov Theatre Studio resembled the First Studio's 1914 exercises in the production of Prana rays. The exercises in Significance teach the performer to endow other objects or things with the actor's special radiation. Likewise, in the Sustaining exercises, the actor practices "sustaining," or holding, the Radiation.

46. Walking in a circle, let your inner soul radiate from your chest. Send out the invisible rays from your fingers and palms. Proudly radiate all the artistic energies from inside of you.

47. Draw an imaginary line across the floor. When you cross it, your activities will intensify. Practice approaching and then crossing the line. Now, instead of crossing the line and enacting a movement, stretch out your arms and radiate the movement across the line. Use specific parts of your body—your eyes, your hands, your forehead—to radiate the action. Radiate to specific places across the line.

48. Radiate a Quality and several variations of it. Then radiate a sentence. Lastly, radiate a sentence with a gesture.

49. Radiate an activity at the same time you are performing it. For instance, start to drink from a glass of water. Suddenly radiate the act of drinking as you bring the glass to your lips.

Significance

50. Touch things in a special creative way. Make them and your action Significant. Remember that you must have the feeling that to act is to create. Everything on the stage must be important—Significant.

51. With a partner improvise a short scene. Using only three sentences for your dialogue, try to make every word spoken and heard special and Significant.

Sustaining

52. Say the word, "Yes," so that after you have pro- nounced it, a gesture will follow from it. Then say "No," followed by another movement of the arm and hand. Sustain it. Now turn your head as if your name has been suddenly called.

53. Rise from your chair and continue "getting up" even after you have already stood up. This Sustaining feeling should express itself in a prolonged pause. The actor should never pause on stage without Sustaining the previous moment. To hold or fill a pause one has

to develop this internal ability to continue or sustain the action.

54. Now say the word "what" and go into a long, sustained pause. Try to find enough confidence in yourself so that you can go on sustaining the pause for a long time. Get up and say the word "what" and sustain it.

55. Say "Why are you doing that?" First do it fully and completely while sustaining it. Then say, "Why are you ...?" and stop as if something happened—drop the words, not for yourself, but for the audience. This should not give the uncertain feeling that you have just forgotten your lines. It should be as if something essential still lingers and follows the words.

ENSEMBLE WORK

56. Form a circle and realize that there are other persons with you. Each one must open his heart to his partners. Take the hands of those around you and realize the presence of others in the circle. Now drop hands. Paradoxically, the lack of physical contact should increase the feeling for the others.

57. As a group, lift up an invisible golden hoop. Hold it over your heads and carefully put it down in unison.

58. *Wrestling Without Muscles:* Pairing off into couples, each unit should slowly and expressively wrestle. Each student's sense of balance and careful movement should make the wrestling appear like a slow-motion dance.

SENSE OF STYLE

59. Using the memory of your last dream, develop a new style in acting.

60. In a circle, pass a chair to your partner, who will pass it to the person nearest him. Each time the chair completes a cycle, it should be done in a new style, beginning with tragedy, then melodrama, comedy, farce, and clowning.

CHAPTER SIX

STANISLAVSKY'S ANALYTICAL PERIOD: THE TABLE WORK

Stanislavsky's nature was, indeed, a passionate and a complex one. It unfolded itself before us through the years. For a long time it was impossible to grasp much of what was going on within him, thanks to the contradictions which perpetually astonished us. Stencilled definitions of a single color were never applicable in any characterization of him.

Vladimir Nemirovich-Danchenko, 1936

THE MOSCOW ART THEATRE'S 1923-24 TOUR

Invited by the American impresario and producer, Morris Gest, the MAT began its first post-revolutionary tour in September 1922. Leaving Nemirovich-Danchenko behind to keep the studio theatres running, Stanislavsky set out with much of the full MAT company on a major tour that took them to Berlin, Prague, Zagreb, Paris, and the United States. The Soviet authorities saw the MAT trip abroad as a welcomed opportunity to promote their new international image of moderation. Guaranteed advanced sales from the productions were also a means for the nearly bankrupt workers' state to bring in some hard Western currency. For Stanislavsky, the tour also meant a chance to rethink some features of his System. Vakhtangov's lingering illness and death, especially after their deathbed reconciliation, troubled Stanislavsky greatly. He began to understand that his resistance to some of Vakhtangov's discoveries may have been more the result of a conflict of generations and tastes rather than any technical or artistic disagreement. Vakhtangov's reformulations of the System would have to be reconsidered.

The 1923-24 European and North American tour was a huge success, the MAT's greatest. Yet neither the Russian-born Gest nor Stanislavsky could have predicted that a theatre troupe, playing in a language that few spectators understood, would be such a sensation in five different countries. Eleven plays from the company's repertoire—including *Czar Fyodor, The Lower Depths, The Cherry Orchard,* and *The Three Sisters*—were staged in 561 performances. Press conferences, meetings with important political and social figures, sold-out performances, extended runs, lavish dinners were the norm in each city. In Prague and in New York, former MAT members, like Richard Boleslavsky, temporarily rejoined the company. But Stanislavsky was shocked and even mildly depressed by the frenzied reception of the MAT in the West. Artistically, the technical conditions in many of the theatres on the tour were severely limited, and public acclaim seemed grossly out of proportion to the audiences' comprehension of the work.

A number of factors, apart from Gest's unfailing genius at public relations, may explain the MAT's triumph abroad. After the Revolution, as hundreds of thousands of White Russian émigrés flooded the capital cites of Central and Western Europe, a rage for Russian style was suddenly in vogue: Russian decor, ballet, music, cabaret, fashion, food, and Gypsy music. For European Communists, leftwing Socialists, and their sympathizers, the MAT represented the New Russia, the workers' paradise. Among intellectuals and theatre people, the MAT's reputation had been established before World War One. In fact, in the sixteen years since the MAT visited Berlin, the company had been transformed from a young and experimental ensemble into a legendary institution with its own patented style and technique. Some American critics labeled it the "First Theatre" of Europe, as if it predated the Comedie Francaise, the Freie Bühne, or a dozen other major European theatre troupes. Finally, the interwar years saw the rise of international interest in foreign and exotic theatre productions. The seemingly endless monetary inflation in Central Europe sent German, Soviet, and White Russian theatre companies westward to Paris, London, and the New World in search of lucrative engagements and new audiences. In order to overcome the problems of language and an unfamiliar repertoire, their programs tended toward the heavily visual and musical, often in a modernist or folkloric setting.

In New York, Stanislavsky discovered that the European clichés about the New World's commercialism and "hard sell" mentality seemed all too true. Retouched photographs and staged newsreel sequences showed Stanislavsky waving to the American masses as he arrived in New York harbor. (A Russian Orthodox priest had been hired to bless him but, mercifully, failed to show.) Jacob Adler and David Belasco —the kings of the Yiddish rialto and Broadway world—and celebrities like Rudolph Valentino and Mayor Jimmy Walker all vied (or were pushed by their agents) to be photographed with the celebrated master. Again, partly due to a sophisticated promotional campaign, the MAT performances sold out night after night. Despite the hoopla, many New York critics comprehended perfectly that a new kind of acting and ensemble work was on display at the Al Jolson Theatre. A few young American actors in the sold-out house were also profoundly influenced. The MAT productions were a turning point in their lives. Some eight years later, they would form the backbone of the Group Theatre.

"My Life in Art"

Entreated by Gest and the writer-translator Oliver Sayler, Stanislavsky agreed in early 1924 to write a technical book on his System for Little, Brown and Co. publishing house at the height of the MAT craze. The editors at Little, Brown were definitely interested, but not in the proposed volume on Russian acting theories. Instead they suggested a book of anecdotes and character sketches. Badly in need of money to pay for his son's medical treatment in Switzerland,

Stanislavsky accepted the assignment with reluctance and proceeded to write his autobiography, *My Life in Art,* during the next six months. According to theatre historian Lawrence Senelick, the MAT's Russian-born American translator, Alexander Koiransky, actually took charge of the project as editor, gathering Stanislavsky's materials, cutting and abridging stories, organizing chapters, frantically shaping his unwieldy notes. The result was the first book length account from the master.

Despite its flaws, *My Life in Art* quickly gained a wide English-speaking readership, as well as a Russian one when it was published in a slightly altered version in Moscow two years later in 1926. Although Stanislavsky's profits from the book's sales were substantial, the entire enterprise disappointed him. *My Life in Art* covered nearly every aspect of Stanislavsky's career except that which was most dear to him—the practical work of the System. Now sixty years old, Stanislavsky had yet to produce a printed record of his method of actor training. And unlike Vakhtangov's *Turandot,* no single production, directed by Stanislavsky, stood as a summation of his System work. Resting at the seashore in Nice, after the arduous tour ended in the summer of 1924, Stanislavsky planned his return to Russia.

MOSCOW HOMECOMING

For Stanislavsky, the Moscow of 1924 was a changed city. During the two years of his absence abroad, the NEP had ushered in a striking era of individual prosperity and freedom of movement. Expensive goods and elite cabaret entertainments were available to anyone with sufficient rubles or dollars. Tens of thousands of NEP men, made wealthy through trade, left the towns and villages of their youth to settle in once-forbidden Moscow. Almost as a simultaneous countermovement, an equal number of ambitious young Communists from the west and south found permits for a Muscovite residency. Two new—and contrary—theatre audiences suddenly appeared: the nouveau riche and the political idealists.

Within a short time, the MAT adapted to the new conditions. After abolishing the MAT satellite studios in 1924, Nemirovich-Danchenko concentrated solely on the repertoire of his Musical Studio. Both in decor and in its emphasis on movement and spectacle, the MAT Music Studio soon resembled its Constructivist competitors in the theatre and dance. This "external madness" had overtaken Russia's performing arts. The notion of an independently creative performer with all "his delicate emotional needs" was parodied in the avant-garde cabarets of Moscow. Omniscient directors, like Meyerhold and Alexander Tairov, now took the center stage and pushed the individual actor out of the theatre's spotlight.

During the 1924-25 season, Stanislavsky reinstituted each of the former studios as independent theatres: the First Studio became the Second MAT, under the artistic leadership of Michael Chekhov; the Third Studio was reinstated as the Vakhtangov Theatre; the Fourth Studio was transformed into the Realistic Theatre; and the Second Studio was absorbed into the MAT itself. Although the Soviets wanted the MAT to stage contemporary political dramas, and now there was even a large audience for them, Stanislavsky reiterated his unbending principle to direct only quality plays, not melodramatic propaganda. Stanislavsky planned a program of MAT revivals and new studio classes.

STANISLAVSKY'S "WORK AROUND THE TABLE"

Beginning in the summer of 1925, a noticeable transformation was taking place in Stanislavsky's teachings. Whereas Affective Memory and other psychophysical exercises were once the centerpieces of his System, he now began to place greater emphasis on textual study for the actor. As long ago as 1909, Stanislavsky realized that the System actor had to take on some of the traditional analytical functions of the director to develop a more independent creation. It was not enough to relax, concentrate, act with faith, and elicit remembered emotions. These merely made the performer a superior tool in the hands of the director. To be a working artist on the stage—that is, to creatively design his own role—the actor must also learn how to read a dramatic script in a new way. Beneath the lines and stage directions lies an underworld of subtext, which, when properly analyzed, provides the actor with all the closeted material vital for his internal and physical activity on stage.

Stanislavsky compared the playscript to the railroad line connecting Moscow to Leningrad. The Salvini, or genius-like, actor can board an express train directly to the old capital because his role comes to him completely and intuitively on first reading. The average performer, however, must take a plodding mail train and stop along the way, get a feel for his part at each station, and then continue up the line until he has fully sampled the textual countryside. Most performers need to be filled with a large amount of detail before the total landscape of their role takes shape. Yet not all the play's information can be digested at once. The road to Leningrad starts in Moscow, and often very short stop-and-go trips must be made before completing the journey.

The Objective

Stanislavsky expounded that each play and each scene can be broken down into stations or steps, called playable Units and Beats. These divisions establish a clear and specific direction for each actor and cast. Moreover, the task of the actor can be mapped out into a clear pattern of Objectives (sometimes translated as obstacles, aims, or problems) taken from the dialogue or subtext of the play. Objectives propel the actor into Action. At every moment, the actor is trying to achieve his stated Objective. Once he completes it, then another, in a continuing string of Objectives, appears. If the attempt fails, another Objective must replace the first. The actor's Objective can be a material goal, like obtaining money that is owed to you from a character. It can just as easily be psychological, like forcing your brother-in-law to apologize publicly to you. The Objective must always lead the actor to Action.

The Action

An Action, according to Stanislavsky, is more than a simple physical activity. It also involves the mind. Every Action requires a strong motivating force, or an Objective, to be complete. To open a door is a simple activity. To open a door in search of a corpse is an Action. In addition, a character—to fully enliven the performer's imagination—must have a larger, overriding desire, called a Through-Action by Stanislavsky, and a goal that take him through the play, called a Super-Objective. Objectives, Actions, Through-Actions, and Super-Objectives must all fit snugly into the playwright's plotline or dramatic theme. This is the network of sidetracks and direct lines that lead to Leningrad.

Stanislavsky's analytical grid revealed to actors the true psychological behavior of a play's characters at any point in the performance. Characters could now be analyzed like living people. Of course, actors before Stanislavsky knew that every Action of a character must be motivated by some force or personal history. But here, Stanislavsky reversed the equation: an actor must first have an Objective, which will determine his Action. For example, seeing an actor standing in an audition line, we could make the following analysis of his activity:

PHYSICAL ACTIVITY: Waiting in an audition line.
OBJECTIVE: Finding work in the theatre.
ACTION: Preparing mentally to audition.
SUPER-OBJECTIVE: Becoming famous as an actor.

THROUGH-ACTION: Being discovered by an important
director in a performance.

Given Circumstances

The key to the actor's choice of Actions and Objectives
are the Given Circumstances set down in the play text. By
focusing on individual scripts, like Griboyedov's *Woe to
Wit* and *Othello,* Stanislavsky painstakingly discussed and
uncovered these with his young performers. To discover the
Given Circumstances, he said, one must take into account
the following: all the facts about the place and era; the past
and future of the characters; the subtext of the dialogue and
stage directions. Once separated and listed, the Given
Circumstances could be converted into character aims and
scored into immediate desires ("I want ..."), which would
assist the actor in deciding what he would do under each
condition faced by his character. All this work was known
as Stanislavsky's "table period" because so much time was
spent around an actual table discussing the play, its parts, the
characters, and their behavior.

This new approach to acting corresponded to Stanislavsky's new primary role as a director. While nearly all the
features of his System had been in place since 1909, an
emphasis on one, or more, essential elements shifted several
times during his last thirteen years. Why Stanislavsky altered his System, in both its theory and in the sequence of its
instruction, is usually explained as a pedagogical failure or
personal dissatisfaction. For some theatre historians, Stan-

islavsky's training methods were merely being refined, progressing, and adjusting themselves. But there are also strong indications that these later modifications in the System are closely linked with social, aesthetic, and career changes as well as personal pressures in Stanislavsky's own life during his final years.

The "Magic If"

From 1916 to 1924, the span of his second period that concentrated on Affective Memory (Sense Memory and Emotional Recall), Stanislavsky was only involved in three new productions. Much of his time was spent on teaching and classroom experimentation. The "work on oneself" was paced according to the slow and steady dictates of the workshop environment. No dire pressures to perform or produce were operative. During his third period, his analytic phase of table work, or the "work on the role," from roughly 1925 to 1928, Stanislavsky directed eight major premieres. While stretched out over weeks and months, the table work brought the actor more immediately into the life and style of the play. Affective Memory exercises for the untutored performer could not be easily inserted into a crowded rehearsal regimen. And even then, such exercises frequently took the young actor's thoughts away from the production itself and into another realm—himself. A quicker and more controllable "bait" lay in the technique of the "Magic If." In each moment of the play, Stanislavsky asked his actor what he would do "if" he were the character. This allowed the actor's imagination to serve the immediate Given Circumstances of the play. And it finally brought the director and actor into a more equal partnership. Besides, the "Magic If" questioning process kept the rehearsals focused on the play and characters.

Tempo-Rhythm

In the summer of 1925, Stanislavsky added new physical acting drills to supplement his textual breakdowns. He called this work Tempo-Rhythm. The musical notion of rhythm always found its way into Stanislavsky's bag of ideas. (He once referred to his own lackadaisical movements as having a "camel" or "dead wave rhythm.") But it was only after his Opera Studio courses (1918-22) and Vakhtangov's death in 1922 that Rhythm became a major theatrical factor. According to Stanislavsky, Tempo refers to the general pace of life that is found in a shared physical or cultural environment. Each nationality, locale, and era has its own unique Tempo or temporal pattern. Rhythm, or the relationship between beats, springs from specific individual activity and varies from person to person. Finding the Tempo-Rhythm of a scene helps the actor determine the measure and timing of each character's action. Along with Tempo-Rhythm, Stanislavsky schooled his actors in a simple form of Justification, which he borrowed from Vakhtangov.

THE RESULTS OF THE TABLE WORK

The result of Stanislavsky's new techniques was clearly seen the very next MAT season in January 1926. His production of Alexander Ostrovsky's *Burning Hearts,* a nineteen-century comedy with a Robin Hood-like hero, amazed everyone. In many ways it resembled Vakhtangov's *Turandot* with its bold musical effects, colorful decor, quick and playful dialogue, strong eccentric movement, and socially satiric mood. Working with young actors, Stanislavsky created what he termed a Gogolian "comedy from within." Each grotesque embodiment was internally supported by the individual performer's private Rhythm and Justification. The Soviet audiences were ecstatic and most critics found it even superior to Vakhtangov's own acclaimed *Turandot.* Stanislavsky's audacious approach to the *Burning Heart* and its modernist settings reminded some reviewers and historians of the best of Meyerhold's productions. At 63, Stanislavsky demonstrated that he was still capable of surprises and risks. He had also learned from his former pupils.

Two other productions followed in rapid succession. At the end of 1926, Stanislavsky staged one of the most controversial Soviet plays of his time, Mikhail Bulgakov's *Day of the Turbins.* A dramatization by Bulgakov of his own novel, the play sympathetically told the story of a doomed Russian bourgeois family during the crisis of the Russian

Civil War. Here for the first time, but without Communist sloganeering, a play unfolded the story of the Revolution's losers, the White Army's supporters, waiting out their last days and hours before the entry of the victorious Red Army. In rehearsals, Stanislavsky created a complicated and dynamic play-score with an "unbroken chain of Objectives and Units" for each actor. Rather than a linear sequence of performance activity, *Day of the Turbins* could be played out as a web of Actions. Both the subject matter and its theatrical handling caused a sensation. The White characters' dramatic and human realities violated Soviet cultural canons and stirred the Moscow audiences. Spectators had only seen two-dimensional presentations of such social villains during a decade of Soviet propaganda plays. Here, anti-Soviet, forbidden thoughts (and not drawn from some distant historical time) were spoken with truth and conviction. In the midst of *Turbins* performances, one could hear spectators' gasps. Some reportedly fainted in their seats. Once again, for a record 103 performances, Stanislavsky became a creator of spectacle.

In 1926 and 1927, Russia's relaxed political and open artistic climate finally soured and hardened. Plays such as Bulgakov's were short-lived and would not be seen again publicly in Moscow until the late 1950s. Like other Soviet theatres, pro-government or fellow-traveling, the MAT had to produce modern Communist plays, based on Socialist Realist aesthetics. Stanislavsky accepted the challenge and in 1927 staged (with Ilya Sudakov) Vsevolod Ivanov's revolutionary melodrama, *Armoured Train 14-69*. Working

closely with only the actors playing the Bolshevik characters, he trained them to personalize their roles and play
against the Soviet stage clichés of one-dimensional infalli-
bility. Conversely, the actors with anti-Soviet parts were
given little internal instruction to develop their characters.
Here Stanislavsky demonstrated his wealth of theatrical ingenuity: the spectators subconsciously identified with the
better, more internalized roles because of the depth of their
characterizations. The anti-Bolshevik and politically neutral
characters, normally the audience's favorites because they
were written with more detail and personality, were acted in
the *Armoured Train 14-69* with external qualities only.
Somehow they appeared less human or interesting than the
Soviet heroes. Now the Soviet authorities praised their new
comrade-director. Anatoli Lunacharsky, the Minister of
Education and Culture, officially welcomed Stanislavsky
into the new era.

In October 1928 at the 30th anniversary of the MAT, after
handfuls of congratulatory telegrams were read, Stanislavsky boldly declared that his theatre would not change its
aesthetic modes to satisfy state directives. Neither he nor the
MAT would be turned into a propaganda organ for the
Communist Party. Stanislavsky announced that the time
was right for him to resume his work as a writer. Since no
practical book had yet to appear on the fundamentals of his
System or his latest discoveries, this one project would now
command his attention. Two days later, while performing
the role of Vershinin in a special performance of *The Three
Sisters,* Stanislavsky suffered a massive heart attack. His

medical condition was serious and he was kept isolated in his bedroom. After several months of forced inactivity, Stanislavsky once again picked up his notebooks and began to draft outlines for his long overdue book on the System. In a letter to his research assistant, Lyubov Gurevich, Stanislavsky openly wondered who his readers would be: experts on the theatre or laymen? The matter would plague him for some time. Meanwhile, plans were made for Stanislavsky to recuperate abroad in the South of France and Germany.

CHAPTER SEVEN

STANISLAVSKY'S WORK ON ACTION AND "PHYSICAL ACTIONS"

What scales, what arpeggi for the development of creative feeling and experience are required by the actor? What exercises resembling solfeggi are needed by him? They must be given numbers for the systematic exercises in the school and at home. All books and works on the theatre are silent on this score. There is no practical textbook.

Konstantin Stanislavsky, *My Life in Art*, 1924

STANISLAVSKY, THE WRITER

In December 1929, Norman Hapgood, a New York journalist, and his wife, Elizabeth, a Russian translator, visited Stanislavsky at a German resort in Badenweiler. They persuaded him to persevere with his technical book and offered to secure for him an American publisher with Elizabeth serving as a translator/editor. Excited by the prospect, Stanislavsky began to assemble more earnestly his various notebooks and papers. Four books, he thought, would comprise the writings on his System with the following titles: 1) Work on Oneself; 2) Work on One's Role; 3) The Creative Mood; and 4) Three Trends in Art, a comparison of his System with traditional procedures in actor training. (Only the first was completed and published in his lifetime.) But Stanislavsky's writing difficulties and blocks instantly reappeared. While he could lecture with force and clarity before a classroom of students or around a table with a cast of actors, Stanislavsky felt at a loss when it came to setting down his words and concepts on paper. Moreover, not knowing how to go about explaining his work in a simple and entertaining manner (especially for the American market), Stanislavsky adopted the format of a fictional dialogue based on Plato's *Dialogues* (c.300 B.C.) and Denis Diderot's *Paradox of the Actor* (1778). The first of the volumes, *An Actor Prepares* (or translated from the Russian, *The Actor Works on Himself*) took some five years to complete. And, like *My Life in Art,* it left Stanislavsky in a state of artistic malaise. The printed words, whether edited by an American translator or Russian assistants, never precisely articulated his technical discoveries.

The writing of *An Actor Prepares* corresponded to a new period (1929-34) in Stanislavsky's thinking. He finally agreed with Nemirovich-Danchenko that his notoriously long rehearsals were unnecessary. The detailed analytical discussions of breaking down a text around a table became an excuse for many actors to procrastinate rather than to do actual work on a production. And so many dramatic concepts, especially the best ones, in the end were irrelevant to the staging of the play. Similarly, Affective Memory, with its direct dependence on the unconscious, could not produce immediate results from inexperienced performers. Stanislavsky looked to Action, what the character must do, and Imagination, how the actor enters into the play's Given Circumstances, as the new springboards of his System. The actor's feelings, Stanislavsky believed, either grew out of the inner motivations for his Actions, or the specific and challenging images produced in the actor's imagination.

As always, the other elements of the System were preserved in Stanislavsky's writings, but their significance had diminished to methods of training, preparation, and embodiment of character. His concern for the physical aspects of his actors' Work on Self and Tempo-Rhythms revealed themselves in the posthumous *Building a Character* (NY, 1948)—or Work on the Role. During this period, Stanislavsky was involved as an Artistic Director in only three completed productions, Othello (mounted by Ilya Sudakov in 1930); an adaptation from Gogol's novel *Dead Souls* (completed under the direction of V.G. Sakhnovsky in 1933); and Ostrovsky's *Artists and their Admirers* (directed by N.N. Litovtseva in 1933).

THE FINAL PRODUCTIONS

During 1929 and 1930, Stanislavsky attempted to direct *Othello* from Nice through long-distance correspondence with Sudakov. Instead of a breakthrough in methodology, however, Stanislavsky's instructions revealed a more complicated desire to integrate all of the MAT's and his own System's techniques into one production. To begin with, Stanislavsky's childhood love for ingeniously built, or trick, properties and historical detail can be seen in page after page of the *Othello* prompt book. In the first production note for Act I, Scene 1, Stanislavsky suggested that the tin oar of the gondolier, bringing Roderigo and Iago to Brabantio's house, be hollowed out and filled with water, creating a suitable and impressive splashing sound for the opening minutes of the production. In other notes, Stanislavsky requested specific fabrics, colors, shapes, and mechanical designs for each prop and stage piece. The size of Desdemona's handkerchief, for instance, became a subject of considerable thought. Stanislavsky's messages to the actors playing Othello and Iago were a curious blend of coaching in Affective Memory (although he claimed otherwise), "Magic If," Textual Analysis, and Action. Yet despite its exacting preparations (157 rehearsals), the MAT production of *Othello* was badly received. Like *Cain*, Stanislavsky's 1920 experiment in expressiveness, *Othello* became so filled with demonstrations of scenic ideas that the production itself and the acting trailed off into tedium. After ten performances, Nemirovich-Danchenko closed it. It never returned to the MAT repertory.

In the fall of 1930, a healthy and vigorous Stanislavsky returned to Moscow. During the days, the master held court in his living room and made notes for his acting books. In the evenings, Stanislavsky watched MAT productions and occasionally participated in rehearsals for new shows and revivals. Seemingly arbitrary changes and reschedulings were ordered by the omnipotent Artistic Director over the silent protests of the young actors and directors. No one dared mention that Stanislavsky's own directorial projects, despite their conceptual brilliance in the long drawn out rehearsal process and their faultless manifestations of his acting System, resulted in less than artistic masterpieces on stage.

The writer Mikhail Bulgakov, a frequent observer of Stanislavsky's critique sessions at the MAT, wrote a satirical roman à clef in 1937 about the master's incessant tinkering with other director's presentations. Posthumously titled in 1965, *The Theatrical Novel* (in English, *Black Snow* [London, 1967]), it presents the Stanislavsky character as a hypochondriac and a crazed genius, who appears at his own theatre exactly twice a year. Then he unnecessarily fusses with each rehearsal and production by interjecting ridiculous invented exercises and études, while a retinue of secretaries, literary historians, dramaturgs, and assistant directors take down his every word. One actor playing the part of an old man, Bulgakov wrote, shyly hands flowers to his beloved during a scene. The fictitious Artistic Director jumps up and begins to lecture the cast about the myriad solutions for best presenting the stage action. He demonstrates various ways for holding flowers and rambles on about the clever choices and assortment of styles that famous performers used to present gifts to their stage partners. Finally, the director demands a bicycle. The stagehands and actors look blankly at each other. No bicycle appears in the play. "Show your love for this woman by riding around her," the Stanislavsky character shouts, as the actor with the flowers wobbles precariously on the bicycle around the frightened actress. After a long series of System-like instructions, the confused performer is told to concentrate only on his beloved as he continues to encircle her with the bicycle. Eventually, the exhausted and abused actor rides out of control past the proscenium edge and falls straight into the orchestra pit. Although an obvious satire, the bicycle scene in Bulgakov's uncompleted book suggested the frustrations and feelings of many MAT observers and members concerning Stanislavsky's interferences in their productions of the early thirties.

THE METHOD OF PHYSICAL ACTIONS

In the end, Stanislavsky's busy days and grueling schedule took its toll on his health, and he returned to his German spas for several months of rest. Back in Moscow once more, in the fall of 1931, he organized a new group of budding disciples and MAT veterans, including the actors Kachalov, Ivan Moskvin, and his young directors, Nikolai Gorcharkov and Mikhail Kedrov. Later the director Vasily Toporkov, and Grigori Kristi and L.P. Novitskaya, in the role of dramaturgs, joined them. Together they plotted a plan for an innovative staging of Alexander Griboyedov's classic satire, *Woe to Wit*. Everything must be converted to Action, Stanislavsky maintained. Action—not Imagination, not Feeling—was the "material" of the actor. In other words, Stanislavsky himself finally agreed that too much time in rehearsal was given over to the actors' preparations. The "work on oneself" and "the work on one's role," which he had pioneered from 1909 until 1931, belonged to the classroom studio where it was taught to beginning MAT actors over a three-year period. Once integrated by working actors, it was no longer part of the production process. The new emphasis on Action was also becoming the main thrust of his partially completed books. Yet Stanislavsky's *Woe to Wit* group, charged with discovering another technique for the convenience and efficiency of the director and his production, went even further in their quest. Their new idea was called the Method of Physical Actions.

Between 1932 and 1936, Stanislavsky's health declined. Much time was spent seeking cures aboard. By 1934 he had practically divorced himself from the daily activities of the MAT. According to many foreign visitors, the acting and the productions at the MAT during this period were the least interesting to be seen in Moscow. Lee Strasberg, reporting on one such trip in 1934, noticed sloppy direction and acting discipline (including performers looking out into the audience) everywhere on the MAT stage, now renamed the Gorky Moscow Art Academic Theatre. Stanislavsky had retreated deeper into preparing his books and workshops. In the summer of 1934, during an annual period of recuperation in France, he coached the American actress Stella Adler in a four-week session on Given Circumstances and Action. Back in Moscow, Stanislavsky opened a new theatre, the School of Opera and Drama, where he tested the Method of Physical Actions, his final refinements of the System.

The term Physical Actions appeared as early as 1916 and was referred to again during the twenties and early thirties. But in 1935 it began to acquire a new meaning. The Method of Physical Actions was intended to be a correlative to the slow motion rehearsal process normally associated with the Stanislavsky System. Without relying on their memories, imaginative powers, or analytical abilities, actors were compelled by the director to decide which Physical Actions they would execute in the Given Circumstances of the play. Only that which could be physically performed and seen by an audience was allowed. Therefore, a character in love could not be acted merely through feeling; a Physical Action had to express it.

Although it appeared to be a purely directorial device—actors were not even informed by the director of the play's intentions and themes until a few days before opening night—in fact, the Method of Physical Actions equally distributed creative responsibilities for the production between the performers and the director. No more could the actor remain passive, waiting for cues and corrections from the omniscient director with his holy prompt book; nor was the director at the mercy of self-inspired performers. The Method of Physical Actions was predicated on a simple discovery that Stanislavsky borrowed from Michael Chekhov and Vakhtangov's followers (who, in turn, were influenced by Meyerhold): all physical action is psychophysical. This means that internal feeling and character identification could be stimulated by pure movement, action, and rhythm.

The Plan of the Method of Physical Actions

In an undated transcription, probably from 1936, Stanislavsky outlined a twenty-five step plan for the director (and indirectly for the performer) incorporating the Method of Physical Actions in the rehearsal process. [A translation of this scheme, although somewhat confused in style, appears in Stanislavsky's *Creating a Role* (NY, 1961).] Below are the directorial steps of the Method of Physical Actions:

1. In the simplest terms, explain the plot of the play to the actors. But do not let them read the play until later.

2. Using the basic Given Circumstances to inspire the actors personally, let them act out the Actions.

3. Let the actors improvise the past and future of the characters.

4. Explain the play's plotline with more details, furnishing more Circumstances and inspiring more "Magic Ifs."

5. Roughly outline the play's Super-Objectives.

6. Have the actors create a personalized Through-Action.

7. Break down the play into large physical Units and Actions.

8. Have the actors perform the Physical Actions with a "Magic If."

9. Still without props, the actors—if necessary—should break the Physical Actions into smaller Units, keeping the logic and continuity of the larger blocks.

10. Through repetition, firmly shape the Physical Actions so they have a logic and believability for the actors.

11. Fix the logic and believability so the actors feel as if the events could actually happen now, at this very minute.

12. Create an active state of "I am" ("It is happening to me") in the improvisation.

13. Each actor now should have absorbed his character's psychology into his own subconscious mind.

14. Let the actors read the play for the first time.

15. As each actor studies the text, have him justify his Actions within the Given Circumstances of the play.

16. Let the actors perform the play, but in place of the dialogue have them practice with the nonsense words "Tra-la-la."

17. The actors should now fix the spoken text within their justified Actions. While they continue to speak "Tra-la-la," ask them to verbalize in their own words the

characters' thoughts. Each actor should inform his partners of his internal monologue. The actors must also visualize the scenic environment.

18. Seated around the table, the actors should now read the playscript to each other. At the same time, but without moving, they should attempt to convey their Physical Actions.

19. This time, moving only their heads and hands to demonstrate their activities, the actors read the play again at the table.

20. Using only rough blocking, have the actors read their parts on the stage.

21. Let the actors discuss their ideas for the mise-en-scène.

22. Explain the actual stage setting. Then let the actors find the appropriate places for their actions.

23. Using any of the four walls as the proscenium arch, test out different stage plans.

24. Discuss the social, political, and artistic meanings of the play.

25. Give the actors any external information—such as habitual gestures and mannerisms—that they have not discovered on their own for their characters.

In the winter of 1938, Stanislavsky started rehearsing one production as a test of the Method of Physical Actions, Moliere's *Tartuffe*. But on August 7, 1938, one-and-a-half years before it would finally come to the MAT stage, Stanislavsky died. *Tartuffe* was staged by Toporkov and Kedrov in 1940. The Method of Physical Actions was embraced by Stanislavsky's last and youngest disciples in the 1940s. Yet its use as a method of actor training was limited by the skill of its teachers. Many of the Method of Physical Actions exercises soon blended with Stanislavsky's final acting experiments, which were delineated in his posthumous writings. These were not publicly known until the publication of Stanislavsky's collected works in 1964. Both inside and outside the MAT acting schools, the efficacy of Stanislavsky's Method of Physical Action is debated to this day.

STANISLAVSKY'S EXERCISES: THE FINAL PERIOD (1929-1938)

Nearly every feature of the Stanislavsky System was being taught in MAT workshops and studios by the early 1930s. Normally, a three-year program introduced students to its basic elements. Exercises and études in Relaxation, Concentration, Naiveté, and some aspects of Action usually took up the first year's work. The other techniques were added in the final two years. Long after their formal period of training ended, however, newly graduated and established actors at the MAT continued their exercise work in the System on a voluntary basis. Much like musicians, they attended open weekly sessions in Concentration, Naiveté, Imagination, and Communication.

Sources for these exercises: *Ilya Sudakov,* Fundamental Elements of the Mastery of Acting *(Moscow, 1934); Stella Adler's 1934 unpublished notes from private sessions with Stanislavsky in Paris; Norris Houghton,* Moscow Rehearsals *(NY, 1936); Konstantin Stanislavsky,* An Actor Prepares *(NY, 1936); Meir Feigenberg,* MXAT *(Copenhagen, 1945); Stanislavsky,* Building a Character *(NY, 1948); Grigori Kristi,* Training Actors in Stanislavsky's School *(Moscow, 1968); L.P. Novitskaya,* Training and Exercises *(Moscow, 1969) and 1976 interviews with Nina V. Kerova.*

213

RELAXATION

1. To create and experience a state of muscular relaxation, you must first bring your body to a maximum state of tension. Inhale and brace your shoulders as if they were carrying a heavy weight. Then slowly exhale as you mentally remove this weight, allowing your shoulders to lower as the burden disappears. Do this with each set of muscles in your body. Inhale deeply, tense the muscles as if a great weight is pressed over or against them, slowly exhale and let the weight drop. (Seated in a chair, you can be checked for relaxation. Your arms, neck, wrists, legs, and ankles should be flexible and limp enough to be easily manipulated by your teacher.)

2. Freely position yourself in a variety of poses. Relax in a pose. Practice using just the right amount of support to keep you balanced in each of the muscular groupings.

3. Practice sending waves of energy from your shoulders to your fingertips and back again.

4. In any position or movement, use a Justification to help you relax and find the proper muscular support. Justify the following movements: 1) throwing your hands out suddenly; 2) stretching your arms up and

down; 3) placing your hands on your shoulders; and 4) making circular gestures before a wall. For instance, when you raise your arms over your head, think of throwing a large ball as you do it. Stretching your arms and fingers forcefully away from your body can be justified as the movement of a hypnotist.

ACTION/GIVEN CIRCUMSTANCES

Action is the core of the actor's art. Not only the movement of his body, but the actor's onstage thoughts and feelings are also Actions. Actions must not violate the Given Circumstances, or scenic conditions, of the text or direction. In fact, the Given Circumstances should motivate the proper Actions from each performer.

5. When the teacher enters the classroom, stand and greet him. This is repeated until all the students rise and speak in unison. Every move and vocalization should be performed without strain.

6. Go up on the stage and sit in a chair. After a period of a few minutes, your teacher will give you the following tasks: 1) calculating the distance between the proscenium arch, 2) solving a mathematical problem, 3) remembering a newspaper story, or 4) spelling the words in a poem. (Sitting on the chair without any

given purpose, facing your class, you probably felt uncomfortable and awkward during the first minutes of the exercise. But once an inner activity was added, strain and self-consciousness should vanish.)

7. Perform as many of the following activities in the shortest amount of time: 1) touch ten different objects in the classroom; 2) spell the name of a city nearby; 3) spell the name of a famous scientist or actor; 4) make comments about the hairstyles and clothes of your other classmates; and 5) tell the class a story that happened to you on this day in another year. At the end of the assignment, remain silent for one to three minutes, releasing all excess energy and tension through mental concentration.

8. Pour a glass of water from a pitcher and give the glass to your teacher. As he names the various pieces of furniture in the room, describe them. List the names of your classmates in alphabetical order.

9. Give your teacher a valuable object that you carry on your body: a watch, wallet, gold ring, etc. Leave the room, so he can hide it. When you return, look for the object, but remember you are to "play" the action as a tragedy. (In order to actually find the object, you, at some point, will probably have to drop the tragic mood to concentrate on the completion of your search.)

Circumstances in the Action

10. Execute one of the following activities: 1) measure your room by walking; 2) scan your room with your eyes; 3) hide something in your room; 4) close your door; 5) enter your room; or 6) move the furniture in your room. Now perform the same activity with a specific purpose. For instance, measure the room by walking because: a) you need to know the square footage of the space because a bedridden child must be brought here; b) you are about to bring some large paintings into this room; c) you are about to exchange your apartment with someone and want to make certain that you are receiving one of an equivalent size. (Having a Justification should give the activity a stronger quality.)

11. Imagine drinking a cup of coffee or tea at the North Pole at 20 degrees below zero Fahrenheit; now imagine drinking it on a very hot summer day when the temperature is nearly 100 degrees.

12. Write a love letter or a condolence letter to a close friend of the family; now write the same letter as a nineteenth-century lady or aristocrat.

13. Walk through the theatre under the following Given Circumstances: 1) before an approaching thunderstorm; 2) with sticky mud on your shoes; 3) avoiding a

snarling mad dog chained to one of the seats; 4) leaving to visit a very ill family member who is expecting you.

14. Shake hands with someone for the following reasons: 1) to show him you are not afraid; 2) to show him that you are not afraid of him; 3) to greet a long lost friend; 4) to show him that you are in love; 5) to meet a prospective in-law.

15. Perform the following Actions with one of the three motivations: 1) Prepare dinner [a) as a chef in a restaurant; b) as a mother trying to please your children; c) as a parent for your sick daughter]. 2) Light a cigarette [a) to chase away mosquitos; b) to enjoy a rare tobacco blend; c) to send a signal]. 3) Look at a newspaper [a) to hide from a passerby; b) to read a review of a production in your theatre; c) to read a friend's obituary].

"MAGIC IF"

The "Magic If" refers to the simple mental process of placing the actor in the immediate Circumstances of his character. An elegant blending of Naiveté, Imagination, and Action, the "Magic If" takes the actor out of the play's intellectual and analytical spheres into the realm of his own individual logic. It inspires a more intense active and inner life onstage.

16. Write a letter, straighten your room, or search for a lost object.   Now add the question of "What If" to the action: i.e., What if I had to straighten my room because very important guests were coming to see me.

17. Using your own logic (and not that of any character's), ask yourself what you would do if you: 1) had to wait for a train, 2) lost all your money, 3) were at home while important people were waiting for you in your office.

18. Act as if you were: 1) in a forest, 2) by a river bank, or 3) in a garden.

19. Act as if you were in your house when a fire breaks out.

20. Act as if you are at home preparing for a crucial university examination to be given the next morning and suddenly the lights go off.

21. Act as if you had to cross a river during a winter storm.

22. How would you act if 1) your handkerchief was a mouse; 2) the box on the table was a frog; 3) the envelope nearby had worms in it; 4) there was a spider on your head.

Combining Given Circumstances and the "Magic If"

23. Notice how the changes in the Given Circumstances and the "Magic If" immediately transform your behavior. 1) Look at an armchair as if you were buying it for your mother. 2) Now look at it as if it were a chair that belonged to Pushkin. Do the same for a piano: 3) as if you were buying it for your club and then as if it belonged to Tchaikovsky.

24. You live at home with your parents. You are hiding from them the fact that you plan to audition for a theatre school in a short period of time. They are about to leave for the theatre to see a show, and this will give you a long, vital, three hours to rehearse. Your parents suddenly cannot decide whether to go to the theatre or not. Then your neighbors arrive and exclaim how much they want the tickets. What do you do?

IMAGINATION

25. Describe, in fine detail, a place with which you are familiar. Who are the people in this place. Explain what you are doing there.

26. Now describe a place with which you are unfamiliar.

27. Imagine that you are an inanimate object like a book or a tree. What do you look like? How do you move? What do you see and hear? Find a Given Circumstance that would cause you to move emotionally and incite you to Action. If you are a tree, for instance, maybe someone is coming to chop you down.

28. Imagine how different your classroom is: 1) early in the morning, 2) in the afternoon, 3) at midnight, and 4) during each of the four seasons.

29. Out of nowhere, famous actors come into your room. Explain, imaginatively, how this happened.

30. Using the following words, "mountain," "shoe", and "snow," create a story and perform it.

31. Create an improvisation that uses the following objects, actions, and phrases:

a. Newspaper	To hide	"That's a pity."
b. Book	To throw	"That's for the best."
c. Note	To lie down	"That's stupid."
d. Lottery Ticket	To find	"That's a surprise."
e. Mirror	To peek	"That's fun."

32. Seated in a circle, your class must tell a fantastic story about how they saved a drowning boy on the way to the studio. Each actor must improvise a piece of the story.

CONCENTRATION

33. Carefully examine the walls and ceiling in your room. For 30 minutes, try to notice all the surface imperfections or any other aspect that would hold your attention. Now look at the walls again as if you are about to spend ten years imprisoned here. Increasing your rate of Concentration or alertness, notice all the walls' faults in one minute.

34. Look at an object of some significance, a very fine piece of antique furniture, for instance. Use your imagination to discover its origins. Now describe the object without looking at it.

35. Look at an object of great beauty, like a famous painting. Try to uncover its most unique feature. Now describe the entire object to the class, stressing that feature.

36. Look into your partner's eyes. Describe their color, form, and luminescence.

37. Walk out of the room. Under the instructions of your teacher, return. Now describe all the changes that he has made.

38. Your teacher builds a figure from match sticks. Study it. After he tears it down, reconstruct it perfectly.

39. Spell the names of all the objects within your immediate and far vision.

40. Listen carefully to all the noises outside your building. Try to determine not only the general sources of their origins, but also specific details. (For instance, in which direction is a speeding automobile going, or how many and what kinds of birds are chirping.)

41. Listen carefully to a piece of music. Try to understand the individual character and quality of the work. Determine the composer's nature and state of mind from it.

42. Hold a coin in your palm. Describe its form, size, weight, and value.

43. With your eyes closed, touch a piece of your classmate's clothing. Attempt to guess the student's identity from your touch.

44. *The Shadow:* Attempt to perfectly "shadow" the activities of your partner. (Unlike the second actor in a *Mirror* exercise, the Shadow does not face his partner, but follows him from behind.)

45. Go into the street and observe different human interactions. Try to define the inner conditions, social status, backgrounds, and relationships of the people you see.

SENSE OF TRUTH AND NAIVETÉ

To create a strong sensation of actual life onstage, the actor must first experience a Sense of Truth for himself. Unlike Stanislavsky's earlier work in Naiveté, the Sense of Truth often requires from the actor a realistic feeling for imaginary and minute detail. In some ways, the Sense of Truth work is identical with Stanislavsky's traditional exercises in Sense Memory, but the emphasis here is on sensations that give the actor a stronger feeling for the performance's reality.

Sense of Truth Exercises

46. In the dark, pick up a small object. Try to understand everything about it with your sense of touch.

47. Light a match or cigarette. Repeat the activity until you strongly feel every detail of it. Now perform the activity again without the actual matches or cigarette.

48. Complete the following activities without any actual objects: 1) wash your hair, 2) make tea, 3) shave, 4) comb your hair, 5) put on clothes, 6) sew with a needle, 7) sew on a sewing machine, 8) sharpen a pencil with a knife, 9) play a musical instrument. Create a complete and convincing Action without worrying about the miming of each activity.

49. In a group, count a stack of real money. Repeat the activity using only imaginary coins and bills.

50. Your teacher has informed the class that he has lost an important small object. Everyone looks for it until it is found. Now carefully repeat the Action, this time knowing where the object is. Retain the original sense of urgency and excitement you had when it was originally hidden the first time.

Naiveté

51. Along with your partners, become children in a candy store.

52. You and your classmates become animals: 1) in a house (like birds, cats, and dogs), 2) on a farm, or 3) in a zoo.

53. Become musical instruments in a folk or jazz orchestra.

54. Become figures in a toy shop or living mannequins in a shop window.

EMOTIONAL RECALL

55. Remember all the foods you ate as a child. Describe their flavors and textures. Reexperience the taste of them.

56. Remember the first time you saw an elephant. Describe it in detail. Relive the experience.

57. Remember the house or apartment where you were born or raised. Describe it. Using chairs, mark out its space. Play in it.

58. Remember the first person you ever hated. Describe how you felt about him. Relive a reaction of seeing him again in your past.

59. Remember how you felt going on your first date. Describe and relive it.

60. Remember your first success. Describe and relive it.

61. Remember a time when you went from a freezing place to a warm one. Demonstrate it.

62. Perform the moment when you wrote your first love letter, business letter, and condolence letter.

COMMUNICATION

63. Sing a popular song silently to yourself. At a signal from your teacher, continue to sing it aloud. At a second signal, return to singing it silently.

64.   Invent an argument with your partner. Allow it to grow in intensity. Now continue the argument without speaking or moving your arms or legs.

65.   Continue the argument, but try to radiate your point of view without any movement of your face or body.

66.   Seated, attempt to radiate an idea or image to your partner across the table.

67.   Transmit the image of an object to your partner. Start with words, gestures, and facial expressions. Finally, use only Radiation.

Adjustment Exercises

68.   Three students sit on chairs before the class. Each is supposed to produce one of these moods: jealousy, suffering, and grief. (But without a motive or a Justification, their looks should appear to be artificial.) Each should add a private Justification to produce depth for his mood.

69.   Ask your teacher if you can leave class early. Adjust your approach to his mood that day.

70.   Do the same as above, but this time your teacher is busy and is hardly paying attention to you. So your Adjustment must be doubly forceful.

71. Repeat the above, but add an emotional quality like malice, joy, conflict, despair, pleasure, apathy, or irony.

72. Figure out a way of asking your teacher to pass over an exercise (which has gone stale) and continue on to the next one.

TEMPO-RHYTHM

All human beings are affected by the speed, or pace, of their environments, called Tempo. In addition, each individual has his own Rhythm, or beat. Work in Tempo-Rhythm coordinates and exercises the actor's external and internal processes, so that stage activities (like a worker going to a factory in the morning or coming home at night) have a specific and different physical component in the acting. Although Tempo-Rhythm would seem to belong solely to the actors' physical preparations, it is, in fact, an important stimulus for the actor's feelings and inner state.

73. Perform any of the Action/Given Circumstances exercises to music. Note how the music affects the rhythm of your actions.

74. Put a metronome on a slow setting. Clap to its beat. Then complicate the exercise, by clapping on every other beat.

75. To the beat of the metronome, place small objects on a tray. Then walk with the tray to the beat and remove the objects.

76. Choose two other actors: one moves slowly, the second moderately, and the third quickly to the sound of three different metronomes. You are all performers who are preparing yourselves, during an intermission, before the last act of a play. The slow-moving one does not appear in the final act and is preparing for the curtain call. The other two are touching up their makeup and costumes, the second performer for an early entrance, and the third for a late entrance in the upcoming act.

77. Using three metronomes, each with a different speed, dress for an evening performance. To the slow beating metronome, recite your memorized text. Express your anxiety by pacing to the moderate one. Finally, quickly dress to the sound of the fastest metronome.

78. Perform the above exercises without a metronome.

79. Substitute a flashing light source for a metronome.

80. Choose a scene and perform it ten times (on a scale of ten speeds), according to the changing rhythm of your character. Begin with Rhythm #5, the rhythm of everyday life. Then vary the scene with slow and fast

rhythms. (For instance, Rhythm #1 belongs to a person nearly dead. Rhythm #9 is that of a man seeing his house on fire. Rhythm #10 is that of a man jumping out of the burning house.)

GLOSSARY OF TERMS

Stanislavsky, Sulerzhitsky, Vakhtangov, and Chekhov invented their own specialized vocabularies, which include many expressions that have since entered into contemporary acting terminology. Some of their neologisms, however, have created untold problems for translators, teachers, and students. Worse still, over the years, the original definitions of these words have been altered or have been replaced by other concepts and phrases. Below are simple descriptions and standard definitions from the acting vocabularies of each of the four teachers. In brackets is the person most identified with the use of the term and a suggested date of its earliest appearance in his teaching, beginning in 1906. Terms that appear in boldface are cross-referenced to other words in this glossary and in the exercises themselves.

—Editor

ACTION
[See **OBJECTIVES AND ACTIONS**.]

231

ADJUSTMENT

[Vakhtangov, 1919] Also known or translated as ADAPTATION. A secondary physical activity or **JUSTIFICATION**, the Adjustment allows the actor to follow direction while maintaining the reality of his character and environment. For instance, in the role of a man caught in a boarding house fire, the actor's first impulse might be to leap anywhere to get away from the fire, even jumping off the stage. A mental Adjustment that the orchestra pit is filled with burning lava keeps the actor on the stage and increases his feeling for the character's predicament.

AFFECTIVE MEMORY

[Stanislavsky, 1909; Vakhtangov, 1918] Normally divided into **SENSE MEMORY** and **EMOTIONAL RECALL**. Affective Memory is the practice of producing controlled feelings and emotional reactions in the actor. By remembering simple visceral sensations (Sense Memories), like the melting of snow flakes on his face, the actor learns to reexperience a past feeling in the present. More complicated emotions, like love, anger, or fear, are stimulated through recalling the vivid instances from the actor's own life (Emotional Recall). The key to Emotional Recall can be found first in a Sense Memory. Instead of recollecting his memories directly, or in story form, the actor recalls the individual sensory details, or the experience's imprints. This allows the actor to control or direct the remembered emotion and bring the feeling into the present tense.

ATMOSPHERES

[Chekhov, 1920] Atmospheres are sensory mediums, like fog, water, darkness, or confusion that are radiated from environments and people. Onstage, the heightened mood of Atmospheres fills the theatre and unconsciously affects both performer and spectator as its unseen waves are absorbed by the actor and radiated out to the audience. Although they cannot be seen, Atmospheres can be felt strongly and are a primary means of theatrical communication. The Atmosphere of a Gothic cathedral, a hospital, or a cemetery influence anyone who enters those spaces. They become enveloped in the Atmosphere. People also give off personal Atmospheres of tension, hate, love, fear, foolishness, and so forth. The play or director suggest the Atmosphere of a scene, and the performers work together to create and maintain it. In Chekhov's studios, Atmospheres took the place of **AFFECTIVE MEMORY**.

BEATS
Also known as **UNITS** or EPISODES. [See **UNITS**.]

CENTERS
[Chekhov, 1931] Every character has a Center. This is the imaginary area inside or outside his body that divides his body and leads him forward. For instance, a proud character can have a Center in his chin or neck. The Center may be any shape or size, color or consistency. A single character may even have more than one Center. Finding a character's Center can lead to understanding his entire personality and physical makeup.

CIRCLE OF ATTENTION
[See **CREATIVE CIRCLE**.]

COMMUNICATION
[Stanislavsky and Sulerzhitsky, 1906] Also known as COMMU-NICATION WITH AN AUDIENCE, CONTACT WITH THE AUDI-ENCE, and, sometimes, **RADIATION**. Acting is a special form of artistic Communication. To go beyond the playwright's words, an actor must learn to deliver a deeper, living message to the audience. This cannot be accomplished through words alone or through a direct contact with the spectator. Instead, the actor communicates or radiates a subtext of thoughts and feelings to his partners, which then, in turn, affects the audience. Facial expressions, movement, and vocal tone are

the normal means of creating character interaction outside the overt meanings of the dialogue. Radiation of **PRANA** rays, directly from the actor's being, however, can be the most intense form of Communication.

CONCENTRATION
[Stanislavsky, 1906] Also translated and known as ATTENTION, CONCENTRATION OF ATTENTION, and INTEREST. The development of the actor's ability to focus or concentrate on a single sensation or object is the first step necessary in producing the **CREATIVE STATE OF MIND**. By concentrating on an object, the actor learns to make himself become interested in it. This, in turn, takes his attention away from the audience, leading him directly and unerringly into the on-stage reality. Even more than Stanislavsky, Vakhtangov believed that an actor must have an object of Concentration every moment that he is on the stage.

CREATIVE CIRCLE
[Stanislavsky and Sulerzhitsky, 1908] Also known as THE CIRCLE, **CIRCLE OF ATTENTION**, and CIRCLE OF LIGHT. An exercise concept in increasing the areas of **CONCENTRATION**, the Creative Circle trains the actor to become acutely aware of his immediate surroundings. He must concentrate only within the imaginary circle around him. The Circle can gradually grow in size from a three-foot circumference around the actor's body to a circle engulfing the entire stage.

CREATIVE STATE OF MIND
[Stanislavsky, 1906] Also known as the CREATIVE SPIRIT and CREATIVE MOOD. The Creative State of Mind is the end product of all the System's exercises. It is the ineffable artistic condition that frees the body of tension and energizes the creative faculties. Actors who achieve it produce a physical ease and concentrated portrayal of character

that is immediately sensed by the audience. Stanislavsky believed that the Creative State of Mind is naturally produced by children at play and by great performers who instinctively intuit their stage roles.

DIVIDED ATTENTION
[First Studio, 1915] Onstage, actors are placed in situations where they must react to or perform several activities simultaneously. Exercises in Divided Attention test the actor's ability to concentrate in the midst of constant distractions. They equally train him to perform one mental activity while executing a second physical task.

DIVIDED CONSCIOUSNESS
[Chekhov, 1928] At first, Chekhov thought of Divided Consciousness as a mystical sensation that occurs when the actor is both aware of his audience and the invisible presence of his living character. At his studios in exile, Divided Consciousness referred to the actor's ability to watch himself from the audience's point of view while he performs on stage.

EMOTIONAL RECALL
Also translated or known as EMOTION MEMORY, EMOTIONAL MEMORY, and REMEMBERED EMOTIONS. [See **AFFECTIVE MEMORY**.]

EURHYTHMY
[Chekhov, 1920] A dance-movement form invented by the spiritualist Rudolf Steiner in Germany before World War One, Eurhythmy has spiritual, aesthetic, and therapeutic values and functions. Through the abstract movement of the human body, Eurhythmy communicates unspoken words, colors, sounds, moods, rhythms, and ideas. A highly coded system with a specific vocabulary of gestures, Eurhythmy is an attempt to express the eternal soul of the performer through outward images and motion. Like the nineteenth-century French philosopher

Francois Delsarte, Steiner trisected movement into Will, Thought, and Feeling.

FANTASY

[First Studio, 1915]   Fantasy results from the marriage of **IMAGINATION** and **NAIVETÉ**. Fantasy involves the ability to imagine, or go beyond, the everyday, realistic world. To fantasize fully, an actor must not only imagine his new creation, but also believe strongly in its existence. Children naturally fantasize about other worlds and beings, but adult actors need to justify these otherworldly beliefs.

FEELING OF EASE

[Chekhov, 1920]   The Feeling of Ease is Chekhov's substitution for Stanislavsky's **RELAXATION** technique. As a directive, it produces outward and immediate sensations in the actor. The Feeling of Ease works on the performer's visceral, private imagery and avoids the intellectual, conscious process of interpreting a command. For instance, the actor can be asked "to sit with a Feeling of Ease," rather than be told by the director "to relax." According to Chekhov, the actor can quickly perform the first command, but must stop and think about the second one.

FEELING OF THE WHOLE

[Chekhov, 1920]   An artistic creation must have a finished form: a beginning, a middle, and an end. Equally, everything on the stage must convey this sense of aesthestic wholeness. This Feeling of the Whole is strongly felt by an audience and must become second nature to the performer. The Feeling of the Whole can apply to an entire production, a scene, or a single monologue.

"THE FOUR BROTHERS"

[Chekhov, 1931]   "The Four Brothers" refers to four linked psychophysical movement skills: 1) the **FEELING OF EASE**, which produces the natural relaxed state that we associate with an accomplished acrobat or athlete; 2) the Feeling of Form, which trains the actor to become an outside creator of his body movement, like a choreographer or sculptor; 3) the Feeling of Beauty, which brings the actor into the sphere of pure motion and being, like a dancer; and 4) the **FEELING OF THE WHOLE**, which helps the actor find the aesthetic controls over the total development of a scene or character, like a playwright or painter.

GIVEN CIRCUMSTANCES

[Stanislavsky and Sulerzhitsky, 1914] Also translated or known as CIRCUMSTANCES and OFFERED CIRCUMSTANCES. An actor must always take into account the Given Circumstances of the play and the director's interpretation of them. This means that the actor must begin studying his part with a knowledge of the play's historical era, its precise time and place, the psychological background of his character and those of his partners', the director's instruction, and the actual mise-en-scène of the production itself.

THE HIGHER EGO

[Chekhov, 1928] The individual performer is always limited by his past experiences and habitual way of doing things. But the actor can learn to break out of his own private patterns and choices. Appealing to the Higher Ego, the source of all artistic energy, allows the actor to temporarily leave his personality behind and expand his range of theatrical ideas and physical activity. From the Higher Ego comes the inspiration to create new and surprising characters.

IMAGINARY BODY

[Chekhov, 1928] To create characters with different physical features from his own, the actor must first visualize an Imaginary Body. This Imaginary Body belongs to his character but the actor can learn to inhabit it. Through constant practice, the performer can change the length and shape of his body and physically transform himself into the character.

IMAGINATION

[First Studio, 1912] Nearly all acting is the result of the performer's ability to imagine and reproduce the reality of a play's fiction on stage. Imagination, for the First Studio's members, took on a special, more intensive meaning. They linked it to **NAIVETÉ** and **AFFECTIVE MEMORY**. In developing their imaginations through game-like exercises, the First Studio actors hoped to overcome the MAT's reputation for solemn, thickly layered acting, punctuated with long, heavy pauses. The quick, spontaneous, "leaps-of-the-imagination" mental and physical activity, natural to children, more closely reflected how they wanted to be perceived in performance. Later, the First Studio members made a distinction between Imagination and **FANTASY**. An actor can imagine anything that he has seen or experienced. But he must fantasize everything else outside his empirical knowledge.

JUSTIFICATION

[Vakhtangov, 1919] Justification is a private or imaginative reasoning that permits the actor to believe strongly in the reality of each stage moment. Although a Justification may be unrelated to the **GIVEN CIRCUMSTANCES** of the play or character, every aspect of the performer's work must be personally justified and truthful. For example, an actor playing Iago must feel jealousy for Othello. According to Vakhtangov's idea of Justification, the actor's true feeling of jealousy can be stimulated from personal sources outside the script. He may, for instance, actually be envious of the star actor playing Othello and justifies Iago's feelings with this simple transference.

" MAGIC IF"

[Stanislavsky, 1912] Also translated as "CREATIVE IF." The "Magic

If" refers to the simple mental process of placing the actor in the immediate **GIVEN CIRCUMSTANCES** of his character. An elegant blending of **NAIVETÉ, IMAGINATION**, and **ACTION**, the "Magic If" takes the actor out of the play's intellectual and analytical spheres into the realm of his own individual logic. It inspires a more intense active and inner life, by asking what would the actor do "if" he found himself in the same dilemma as his character?

METHOD OF PHYSICAL ACTIONS
[Stanislavsky, 1931] Also known as ANALYSIS OF THE METHOD OF PHYSICAL ACTIONS and LOGIC OF PHYSICAL ACTIONS. This is a directorial means of bringing the actor directly into the life of the play. It is predicated on the idea that all Physical Action is psychophysical; movement and thought are inseparable. Through directed improvisational work, the actor discovers the Physical Actions of his character, which leads him into an immediate understanding of the play.

NAIVETÉ
[Stanislavsky and Sulerzhitsky, 1908] Also translated or known as BELIEF, NAIVETÉ AND FAITH, and SENSE OF TRUTH. An inherent human quality, Naiveté is usually lost after childhood. It is ability and desire to believe fully and truthfully in the unseen. To enter into a play's imaginary circumstances, the actor must relearn and develop his childlike powers to completely believe in invisible stimuli.

OBJECTIVES AND ACTIONS
[Stanislavsky, 1920] OBJECTIVES also translated or known as AIMS, GOALS, and PROBLEMS. Each scene of a play can be broken down into the character's Objectives and Actions. The Objective, or what the character wants, propels the actor to execute an Action. This Action normally involves physical and psychological activity that will enable the actor to obtain his Objective. For instance, if the actor's

Objective is to discover a murder, then opening a closet door, a simple activity, becomes an Action when he does it to search for a corpse. And once the actor succeeds in one Action, then another Objective and consequent Action will replace it to form a continuous chain. An actor's **SUPER-OBJECTIVE** and **THROUGH-ACTION** refer to his larger or overriding goal and Action in a play.

PRANA
[Sulerzhitsky, 1906]   Also translated as SOUL RAYS. A Sanskrit word referring to waves of the universal life force. Stanislavsky and Suler believed that invisible rays of Prana could be produced in the hands, finger tips, and eyes of the performer. It can function as a powerful means of **COMMUNICATION** between actors and their audience.

PSYCHOLOGICAL GESTURE
[Chekhov, 1937] The Psychological Gesture is a physical movement that awakens the actor's inner life. It serves as a key to the essential or hidden features of his character. Psychological Gestures may be large or diminutive in size, abstract or natural, but they are always simply executed. A character may only have one Psychological Gesture. For instance, the Psychological Gesture of Hamlet could be illustrated in the far reaching grasp of a man who can only find and hold objects close to him. In performance, the actor need only think of the Psychological Gesture to feed his internal characterization. Whether or not he physically presents the Psychological Gesture onstage has little importance.

PUBLIC SOLITUDE
[Vakhtangov, 1919] The actor's ability to act privately in public is a test of his skills in **RELAXATION, CONCENTRATION,** and **NAIVETÉ.** In this sense, Public Solitude takes the simple work of the **CIRCLE OF ATTENTION** and brings it into a total theatrical environment. It is the actor's first exercise in "living on stage."

QUALITIES
[Chekhov, 1928] Qualities refer to simple feelings or ideas that an actor can express physically, or internal images that he can embody in gesture. Examples are to sit with a Quality of Love, or stand with a Quality of Power.

RADIATION
[See **COMMUNICATION** and **PRANA**.]

RELAXATION
[Stanislavsky, 1906] Also translated as RELAXATION OF MUSCLES and MUSCULAR FREEDOM. One of Stanislavsky's first discoveries was that muscular tension limits the actor's capacity to feel as well as move. A body totally free from tension is essential for stage creativity. According to Vakhtangov, a relaxed performer is better able to follow the precise instructions of his director and not become involved in extraneous, nervous movement. Relaxation and **CONCENTRATION** are often inseparable. Complete attention or absorption on an object, sound, smell, feeling, or thought will automatically free the body of self-consciousness and tension.

RHYTHM
[Stanislavsky, 1906] All human activity follows some rhythmic pattern. Each actor must find the proper Rhythm for his character and all his stage activities. [See also **TEMPO-RHYTHM**.]

SENSE MEMORY
Sometimes known as AFFECTIVE MEMORY. [See **AFFECTIVE MEMORY**.]

SENSE OF LOGIC AND TRUTH
[Stanislavsky, 1921]. Also translated or known as FEELING OF LOGIC and FEELING OF LOGIC, TRUTH, AND CONTINUITY. In

order for the actor to live within his stage reality, he must strongly believe in the simple logic and truth of the **GIVEN CIRCUM-STANCES**. Every **ACTION** must also follow logically from the one before, having, that is, a sense of continuity. Without the Sense of Logic and Truth, the actor cannot feel that he is living in a normal or human environment.

SIGNIFICANCE AND SUSTAINING
[Chekhov, 1931] Significance and Sustaining are active forms of RA-DIATION. Significance exercises teach the performer to endow other objects or things with a unique power. Likewise, in the Sustaining work, the actor practices holding the special power over a word, pose, or object.

SUPER-OBJECTIVE
Also translated as RULING IDEA. [See **OBJECTIVES AND AC-TIONS**.]

TABLE WORK
[Stanislavsky, 1925] Table Work refers to Stanislavsky's intensely analytical period, where he spent much of the rehearsal time with his actors seated around a large table. There, the play's meanings and the character's activities were carefully discussed and investigated.

THE TASK
[Vakhtangov, 1919] The Task resembles Stanislavsky's later ideas of **GIVEN CIRCUMSTANCES** and **OBJECTIVES AND AC-TIONS**. Vakhtangov wanted to combine the actor's separate analytical, psychological, and physical instructions into single playable **UNITS**. The Task of the actor consisted of 1) finding the character's intellectual Goal; 2) feeling the character's physical Desire; and 3) making a stage **ADJUSTMENT** to the demands of the text and director.

TEMPO

[Vakhtangov, 1919]   Like the First Studio's notion of internal **RHYTHM**, Tempo expresses itself in physical activity with the increase or drop of energy. The major difference between Rhythm and Tempo is that the latter derives from the outside environment. In every scene and situation, the actor must find the appropriate Tempo. [See also **TEMPO-RHYTHM**.]

TEMPO-RHYTHM

[Stanislavsky, 1926]   All human beings are affected by the speed, or pace, of their environments, called **TEMPO**. In addition, each individual has his own **RHYTHM**, or beat. Work in Tempo-Rhythm coordinates and exercises the actor's external and internal processes, so that stage activities (like a worker going to a factory in the morning or coming home at night) add a specific and different physical component to the acting. Although Tempo-Rhythm would seem to belong solely to the actors' physical preparations, in fact, it is an important stimulus for the actor's feelings and inner state.

THROUGH-ACTION

Also translated or known as THROUGH-GOING ACTION and THROUGH-LINE. [See **OBJECTIVES AND ACTIONS**.]

THRESHOLD

[Chekhov, 1920]   The Threshold is an imaginary boundary that marks the division between everyday life and the world of the Creative Spirit (See **CREATIVE STATE OF MIND**.). It is symbolized by a line or circle. When the actor crosses it, he has stepped into a magical environment where anything is possible to do or to think. His artistic and spiritual energies can be fully liberated.

UNITS

[Stanislavsky, 1920]   Also known as **BEATS** and EPISODES. Units are the names of the playable divisions or sections of a play. The actor or director breaks down each scene into Units that can be discussed or performed. The Units are to be used only as a rehearsal aid and should not be noticeable to the audience in the final production. The linked Units combine to form **ACTIONS** and **THROUGH-ACTION**.

COURSE AND PROGRAM OUTLINES OF THE SYSTEM

The outlines below are taken from notebook entries, course announcements, journalistic reports, and chapter breakdowns for acting texts. They show the System's transformation (as well as Vakhtangov's and Chekhov's reformulations) in both terminology and emphasis. Adjustments have been made in some descriptions in order to create a format that applies strictly to acting programs. Normally, these outlines constituted two-year programs of intensive work.—Editor

---

SULERZHITSKY'S COURSE ANNOUNCEMENT FOR SYSTEM TRAINING (1914)

[from L.Z. Sulerzhitsky, *Long and Short Stories* (Moscow, 1970)]

I. RELAXATION OF THE MUSCLES

II. CONCENTRATION

III. REAFFIRMING FAITH AND NAIVETÉ

IV. TRANSFORMATION OF THE SELF INTO DIFFERENT CIRCUMSTANCES AND SITUATIONS

V. ESTABLISHING A LIVING OBJECT

VI. AROUSAL FOR HARD WORK

VAKHTANGOV'S COURSE OF STUDY (1919)

[from Vakhtangov's "*Eight Lectures*," given to the author by Lee Strasberg]

I. PREPARATORY WORK
   - A.) Muscular Freedom
   - B.) Concentration
   - C.) Truth, Faith, Justification
   - D.) The Circle of Attention
   - E.) The Task
   - F.) Affective Memory and Emotion
   - G.) Tempos—Increased and Lowered Energies

II. METHOD OF WORK
   - A.) Communication
   - B.) Public Solitude

III. ANALYSIS OF PLAYS AND ROLES

IV. OUTER CHARACTERIZATION

STANISLAVSKY'S ANALYSIS OF THE SYSTEM (1921)

[from *Teatralnaya Kultura* (Moscow, 1921)]

I. RELAXATION OF THE MUSCLES

II. CONCENTRATION

III. AFFECTIVE MEMORY

IV. SENSE OF TRUTH

V. BEAUTY

VI. RHYTHM

VII. FEELING OF LOGIC

VIII. COMMUNICATION WITH AN AUDIENCE

IX. RADIATION

NORRIS HOUGHTON'S DESCRIPTION OF THE MAT TRAINING (1934)

[from *Moscow Rehearsals* (NY, 1936)]

I. PHYSICAL DEVELOPMENT
The actor must be the master of all movement and all the senses.

II. WORK ON ONE'S SELF
   A.) Muscular Freedom and Relaxation
   B.) Circle of Attention
   C.) Imagination and Fantasy
   D.) Affective Memory
   E.) Given Circumstances
   F.) Naiveté
   G.) Communication (Contact)
   H.) Emotional Memory
   I.) Rhythm

III. WORK ON ONE'S ROLE
   A.) "Kernel" of the Role
   B.) Objectives and Actions
   C.) Super-Objective
   D.) Perspective of the Role
   E.) Mastery of the Role

CHAPTER HEADINGS FROM STANISLAVSKY'S *AN ACTOR PREPARES*, WRITTEN IN 1934

[from *An Actor Prepares* (NY, 1936)]

I. ACTION

II. IMAGINATION

III. CONCENTRATION OF ATTENTION

IV. RELAXATION of MUSCLES

V. UNITS AND OBJECTIVES
VI. FAITH AND A SENSE OF TRUTH
VII. EMOTIONAL MEMORY
VIII. COMMUNICATION
IX. ADAPTATION

CHAPTER HEADINGS FROM STANISLAVSKY'S *BUILDING A CHARACTER*, WRITTEN IN 1935

[from *Building a Character*, (NY, 1948)]

I. DRESSING THE PART
II. CHARACTERS AND TYPES
III. MAKING THE BODY EXPRESSIVE
IV. PLASTICITY OF MOTION
V. RESTRAINT AND CONTROL
VI. DICTION AND SINGING
VII. INTONATIONS AND PAUSES
VIII. ACCENTUATION: THE EXPRESSIVE WORD
IX. PERSPECTIVE IN CHARACTER BUILDING
X. TEMPO-RHYTHM IN MOVEMENT
XI. TEMPO-RHYTHM IN SPEECH
XII. STAGE CHARM

L.P. NOVITSKAYA'S ANALYSIS OF MAT TRAINING (1935-1967)

[from L.P. Novitskaya, *Training and Exercises* (Moscow, 1969)]

I. RELAXATION OF THE MUSCLES
II. ACTION/"MAGIC IF"/GIVEN CIRCUMSTANCES

III. IMAGINATION

IV. CONCENTRATION

V. FEELING OF TRUTH, LOGIC, AND CONTINUITY

VI. NAIVETÉ

VII. EMOTIONAL RECALL

VIII. COMMUNICATION

IX. CHARACTERIZATION

X. TEMPO-RHYTHM

XI. MISE-EN-SCENE

XII. UNITS, SUPER-OBJECTIVES, AND THROUGH-ACTIONS

CHAPTER HEADINGS FROM MICHAEL CHEKHOV'S 1942 TEXTBOOK

[from the unpublished book *To the Actor* (1942) and the Russian-language *On the Actor's Technique* (NY, 1946)]

I. IMAGINATION AND CONCENTRATION

II. THE HIGHER EGO

III. ATMOSPHERES AND QUALITIES

IV. PSYCHOLOGICAL GESTURE

V. THE ACTOR'S BODY

VI. INCORPORATION AND CHARACTERIZATION

VII. OBJECTIVES

VIII. RADIATION AND SIGNIFICANCE

IX. ENSEMBLE

X. SENSE OF STYLE

XI. COMPOSITION OF PERFORMANCE

SELECTED BIBLIOGRAPHY

GENERAL

Cole, Toby, editor. *Acting: A Handbook of the Stanislavsky Method* (NY, 1948).

Edwards, Christine. *The Stanislavsky Heritage* (NY, 1965).

Munk, Erika, editor. *Stanislavsky and America* (NY, 1966).

Special Issues of *The Drama Review* T25 (Fall 1964) & T26 (Winter 1964).

Special Issue of *Theatre Journal* (December 1984).

STANISLAVSKY: BIOGRAPHY & EARLY WORK

Benedetti, Jean. *Stanislavsky: An Introduction* (London, 1982).

Magarshack, David. *Stanislavsky: A Life* (London, 1951).

Polyakova, Elena. *Stanislavsky* (Moscow, 1982). Translated by Liv Tudge.

Senelick, Laurence. *Gordon Craig's Moscow "Hamlet"* (Westport, CT, 1982).

Stanislavsky, Konstantin. *My Life in Art* (NY, 1924; Moscow, c.1958). Translated by J. J. Robbins (1924) and G. Ivanov-Mumjiev (1958).

_____. *"The Seagull" Produced by Stanislavsky* (NY, 1958). Edited and introduced by S. D. Balukhaty; translated by David Magarshack.

_____. *On The Art of the Stage* (NY, 1961). Translated and introduced by David Magarshack.

_____. *Selected Works* (Moscow, 1984). Translated by Vladimir Yankilevsky.

EVGENI VAKHTANGOV

Gorchakov, Nikolai. *Vakhtangov School of Stage Art* (Moscow, 1965). Translated by G. Ivanov-Mumjiev.
Vakhtangov, Evgeni. *Notes and Diaries* (Moscow, 1982). Translated by Doris Bradbury.

MICHAEL CHEKHOV

Chekhov, Michael. *To the Actor* (NY, 1953).
_____. *Lessons for the Professional Actor* (NY, 1985). Introduced by Mel Gordon.
Special Issue of *The Drama Review* T99 (September 1983).

STANISLAVSKY: LATER YEARS

Stanislavsky, Konstantin. *An Actor Prepares* (NY, 1936). Introduced by Sir John Gielgud; translated by Elizabeth Hapgood.
_____. *Building a Character* (NY, 1948). Introduced by Joshua Logan, translated by Elizabeth Hapgood.
_____. *Stanislavski Produces "Othello"* (NY, 1948). Translated by Helen Nowak.
_____. *Creating a Role* (NY, 1961). Translated by Elizabeth Hapgood.
Gorchakov, Nikolai. *Stanislavsky Directs* (NY, 1954). Translated by Miriam Goldina.
Toporkov, Vasily. *Stanislavski in Rehearsal* (NY, 1979). Translated by Christine Edwards.